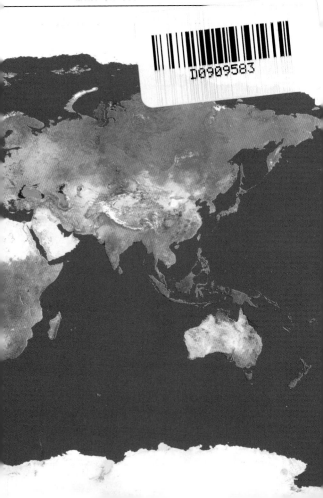

# THE MINI
# Satellite
# Atlas
## OF THE
# WORLD

*Credits*

*The Mini Satellite Atlas of the World*
*English Language Edition*

*Publisher*
AND Cartographic Publishers Ltd, Finchampstead, United Kingdom

*Consultants*
Simon Butler
Peter Sackett
Robert Stacey
Emery Miller
Edith Stacey

*Production of Satellite imagery*
Robert Stacey, WorldSat International Ltd., Mississauga, Ontario, Canada;
Jim Knighton

*Satellite Data NOAA*
Ocean Floor Bathymetry by NOAA courtesy of USGS
Images on pages 14,15,16,17,26,27,28 and 29 based on the Resurs satellite
imagery, provided by SSC/Satellitbild of Kiruna, Sweden
Digital image processed on a Silicon Graphics workstation using PCI
EASI/PACE software

*Cartographic Design, Layout and Production*
AND Map Graphics Ltd, Finchampstead, United Kingdom

*Printing and binding*
Editoriale Libraria, Trieste, Italy

© 1998 AND Cartographic Publishers Ltd
© 1998 WorldSat International Ltd
© 1998 SPOT Image

ISBN: 0 9533246 0 5

# Foreword

*The production of this Atlas brings a new era in map reproduction to the world. An era where we can not only look at the boundaries that are delineated by the cartographer but also the underlying reality. In the process of creating this reality it was necessary to further enhance the imagery that went into the construction of the atlas. We matched elevation data for the entire earth to the space imagery and generated shaded relief which imparts a sense of the third dimension to the final maps. We incorporated relief data on the ocean floor so that you could peer through the water with your 'X-ray eyes' and study the variations in terrain (or elevation) that exist under our vast oceans. This in deference to the 'other' two-thirds of our world. Finally, we have incorporated the traditional cartography, delineating the non-visible components (the ether - so to speak) of our World, such as political boundaries, as well as putting place names to towns and regions to provide an all-encompassing perspective of our new earth as it moves us inexorably into our next millennium.*

# Contents

Key to symbols 5

Index to map pages 6 –7

Technical section on Satellite Mapping 8 –10

Europe 1:43,750,000 12 –13

British Isles 1:7,500,000 14 –15

Belgium and The Netherlands 1:5,000,000 16 –17

Scandinavia & The Baltic States 1:12,500,000 18 –19

European Russia 1:22,500,000 20 –21

Poland, Czech Republic, Slovakia & Hungary 22 –23

Germany 1:5,625,000 24 –25

France 1:7,500,000 26 –27

Spain and Portugal 1:7,500,000 28 –29

Alpine States 1:5,625,000 30 –31

Italy 1:7,500,000 32 –33

Balkans 1:7,500,000 34 –35

Greece and West Turkey 1:7,500,000 36 –37

Turkey 1:12,500,000 38 – 39

Middle East 1:27,500,000 40 –41

Israel, Jordan and Lebanon 1:6,250,000 42

The Gulf States 1:12,500,000 43

Africa 1:65,000,000 44 –45

Northwest Africa 1:25,000,000 46 –47

Northeast Africa 1:25,000,000 48 –49

West Africa 1:25,000,000 50 –51

Central Africa 1:25,000,000 52 –53

Southern Africa 1:25,000,000 54 –55

Asia 1:71,250,000 56 –57

Northwest Asia 1:30,000,000 58 –59

Northeast Asia 1:30,000,000 60 –61

Southern Asia 1:25,000,000 62 –63

Southeast Asia 1:25,000,000 64 –65

China 1:25,000,000 66 –67

Japan and Korea 1:12,500,000 68 –69

Malaysia and Indonesia 1:25,000,000 70 –71

Oceania 1:87,500,000 72 –73

Australia 1:30,000,000 74 –75

New Zealand 1:10,000,000 76 –77

North America 1:75,000,000 78 –79

Canada 1:30,000,000 80 –81

United States 1:33,500,000 82 –83

Northwest USA 1:15,625,000 84 –85

Northeast USA 1:15,625,000 86 –87

Southwest USA, Alaska,Hawaii 1:15,625,000 88 –89

Southeast USA 1:15,625,000 90 –91

Central America and Caribbean 1:35,000,000 92 –93

South America 1:60,750,000 94 –95

South America, (North) 1:35,000,000 96 –97

South America, (South) 1:35,000,000 98 –99

Polar Regions 1:110,000,000 100

Global Facts and Figures 102 –109

Satellite Images from around the World 111 –147

Glossary to names 148

How to use the Index 149

Index to Names 150 -160

World Physical (Atlantic centred) Front Endpaper

World Physical (Pacific centred) Back Endpaper

# Key

| | |
|---|---|
| | National Boundary |
| | State Boundary |
| | Undefined or Disputed Boundary |
| Ottawa | National Capital |
| Winnipeg | State Capital |
| NEW YORK | Town/City with population > 1 Million |
| Duluth | Town/City with population < 1 Million |
| 3954 ▲ Mt.Robson | Mountain Peak with height in metres |
| CANADA | Country |
| MONTANA | State |
| ROCKY MOUNTAINS | Physical Region |
| ATLANTIC OCEAN | Ocean |
| Lake Superior  St. Lawrence | Lake, River |
| NEWFOUNDLAND | Island |
| Hudson Bay | Gulf, Strait |
| Cape Sable | Cape, Point |

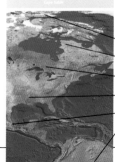

— Glacier, Ice cap

— Tundra

— Coniferous forest

— Cultivated land

— Desert

— Rain forest

# Index to Map Pages

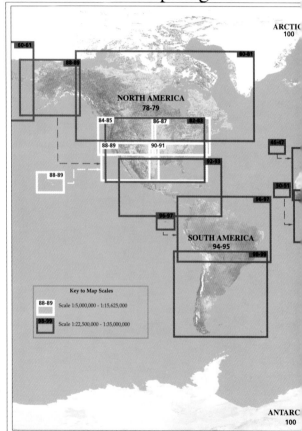

ARCTIC
100

60-61

88-89

80-81

**NORTH AMERICA**
**78-79**

84-85 | 86-87 | 82-83

88-89 | 90-91

46-47

88-89

50-51

92-93

96-97

96-97

98-99

**SOUTH AMERICA**
**94-95**

98-99

**Key to Map Scales**

88-89  Scale 1:5,000,000 - 1:15,625,000

98-99  Scale 1:22,500,000 - 1:35,000,000

ANTARC
100

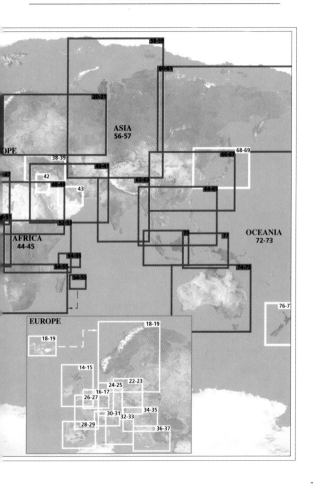

7

# Satellite Mapping

The images in this Atlas have been created by processing signals gathered in space by satellites circling the Earth in near polar orbits.

Sensors on the satellite register different kinds of electromagnetic energy emitted or reflected from the Earth's surface. This data is collected digitally and transmitted to ground stations where it is compiled into digital images. These images can then be used to create products such as the pictorial images in this Atlas.

**Maps as Interpreted Images of Earth:**

Satellite imagery and image analysis provide the ability to extract many different data sets from a single source. Not only can it be used in the generation of maps as seen in traditional atlases or as

combined imagery and cartography, as seen in this atlas, but it can also be used to extract vegetation and land cover information.

### Landsat Satellite:

The American Landsat satellites (left) were the first satellites to make space imagery available to the general public. These satellites are based on one of two specific instruments, respectively referred to as 'MSS' (Multi-Spectral Scanner) and 'TM' (Thematic Mapper) imagers. The MSS scanner collects data in 4 bands (or regions) of the electromagnetic spectrum and the TM imager expands this capability by acquiring data in 7 bands.

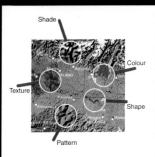

### Interpreting Satellite Images:

The ability to interpret satellite imagery falls into three basic categories: 1) visual interpretation, as in photography; 2) analysis of the spectral content of the imagery as noted under 'image analysis' and 3) texture and pattern analysis. Texture and pattern analysis is relatively new and promises to significantly enhance the capabilities of the whole 'image analysis' process.

The ability to extract specific information is dependent on the particular characteristics of the satellite. Each type of satellite is configured differently and each configuration has strengths that will determine the specific application for which the satellite is best suited.

## The Final Touches:

The ultimate differences in maps derived from the same source can be found in the 'artistic license' that is applied by the cartographer. This encompasses such issues as whether or not to apply shaded relief, highlighting terrain variations and imparting a sense of 3-D to the image. In the case of this atlas we chose to apply ocean floor relief (derived from NOAA's ETOPO-5 files) allowing us to view through the water and visualise the continuous geological structures of our Earth. The artistic license applied in this atlas is 'reality', bringing the reader closer to a true view of our planet.

## The Orbit and Sensor Characteristics of NOAA's AVHRR:

The Advanced Very High Resolution Radiometer (AVHRR) refers to the specific sensor aboard the National Oceanographic and Atmospheric Administration's (NOAA) polar orbiting environmental satellites (as different from the GOES - Geostationary Orbiting Environmental Satellites). The AVHRR based satellites are

primarily designed for monitoring and forecasting weather, following a sun-synchronys orbit at a height of 833 kilometres and circling the Earth 14 times a day (102 minutes/orbit). During each passage the imager picks up a ground track that is 2399 km wide (see diagram) and registers pixels that are 1.1 km x 1.1 km. The AVHRR imager collects data in 5 electromagnetic bands as indicated in the diagram below.

| band | wavelength in µm | applications |
|------|------------------|--------------|
| 1 | 0.58 - 0.68 | cloud (day) / surface mapping |
| 2 | 1.725 - 1.10 | surface water delineation, ice and snow melt |
| 3 | 3.55 - 3.93 | sea surface temperature, night-time cloud mapping |
| 4 | 10.30 - 11.30 | sea surface temperature, cloud mapping (day and night) |
| 5 | 11.50 - 12.50 | sea surface temperature, cloud mapping (day and night) |

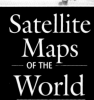

# Satellite
# Maps
## — OF THE —
# World

Eighty-nine full colour satellite
maps covering the entire world
from Pole to Pole, each map
interpreted and enhanced with
elevation data and overlaid with
cartographic detail.

# Europe

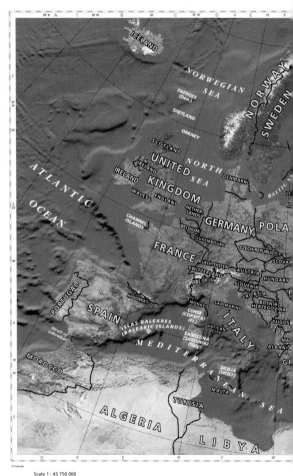

Scale 1 : 43 750 000

0    250    500    750    1000 km

© Copyright

# The British Isles

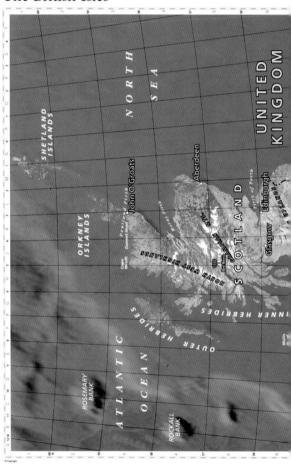

Scale 1 : 7 500 000

0    50    100    150 km

# Belgium and the Netherlands

Scale 1 : 5 000 000

0    50    100 km

WADDENEILANDEN
WADDENZEE

en Helder
IJssel-
meer
THERLANDS
Lelystad

Haarlem
avenhage
(Den Haag)
he Hague)
Amsterdam
Utrecht

Rotterdam
Nijmegen
Arnhem

Tilburg

Eindhoven

Antwerpen

BRUXELLES
BRUSSEL
(BRUSSELS)

LGIUM
Liège

ns
Namur

Charleroi

Bastogne

Arlon

eims

y
Verdun

Groningen
Papenburg

Oldenburg
Bremen

Hoogeveen

Osnabrück

Bielefeld

Münster
Paderborn

GERMANY
Duisburg
Essen
Bochum
Dortmund

Krefeld
Wuppertal

Mönchen-
gladbach
Düsseldorf

Maastricht
Aachen
KÖLN
(COLOGNE)

Bonn

SCHIEFERGEBIRGE

Koblenz
TAUNUS

ARDENNES
RHEINISCHES
Frankfurt
Wiesbaden

LUXEMBOURG
Mainz
Darmstadt

Trier

Mannheim
Ludwigshafen

Luxembourg

Saarbrücken

ARDENNE
Metz
Karlsruhe

Nancy

17

# Scandinavia and the Baltic States

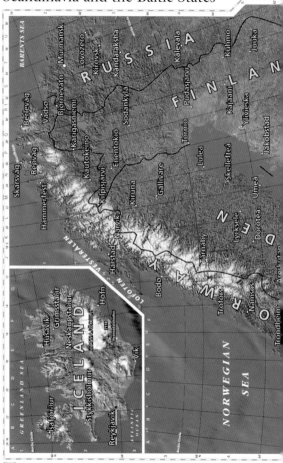

Scale 1 : 12 500 000

RUSSIA

St. Petersburg (ST. PETERSBURG)

Slantsy

Pskov

Valmiera

Daugavpils

Vilnius

Tartu

ESTONIA

LATVIA

Riga

Šiauliai

LITHUANIA

Kaunas

Grodno

Białystok

BELARUS

Helsingfors (Helsinki)

Espoo/Esbo

Tallinn

ÅLAND (AHVENANMAA)

Turku/Åbo

Klaipėda

Liepāja

Kaliningrad

(RUSSIA)

Olsztyn

Uppsala

Stockholm

Norrköping

Linköping

Gdynia

Gdańsk (Danzig)

Elbląg

Toruń

POLAND

Bydgoszcz

Falun

Västerås

Eskilstuna

Örebro

Växjö

BALTIC SEA

Szczecin

Lillehammer

Oslo

Sandefjord

Uddevalla

Göteborg

Jönköping

Helsingborg

Malmö

Ålborg

København (Copenhagen)

Odense

Rostock

Lübeck

GERMANY

HAMBURG

Bergen

Odda

Stavanger

Kristiansand

DENMARK

JYLLAND

Esbjerg

Kiel

Bremerhaven

NORTH SEA

NETHERLANDS

Groningen

0  100  200  300 km

19

# European Russia

Scale 1 : 22 500 000

0    200    400    600    800 km

© Copyright

Dresden

Chemnitz

PRAHA
(PRAGUE)
Plzeň

CZECH REPUBLIC

Salzburg

AUSTRIA

Nürnberg

MÜNCHEN
(MUNICH)

Innsbruck

Augsburg

Main Danube Canal

Frankfurt

Stuttgart

Wiesbaden

Mannheim

Karlsruhe

DÜSSELDORF

KÖLN
(COLOGNE)

Bonn

Freiburg

SWITZERLAND
Zürich

Basel

Aachen

Strasbourg

Mönchen-
gladbach

BELGIUM

Liège

LUXEM-
BOURG

Luxembourg

Saarbrücken

F R A N C E

Nancy

Mulhouse

Scale 1 : 5 625 000

150 km

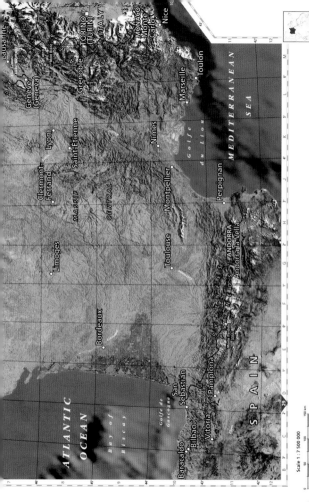

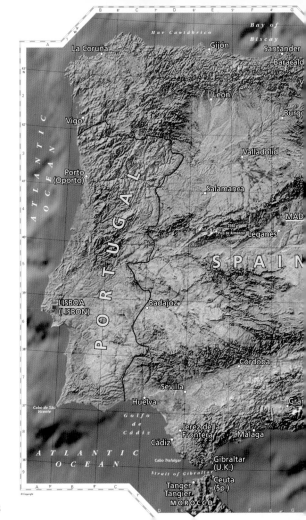

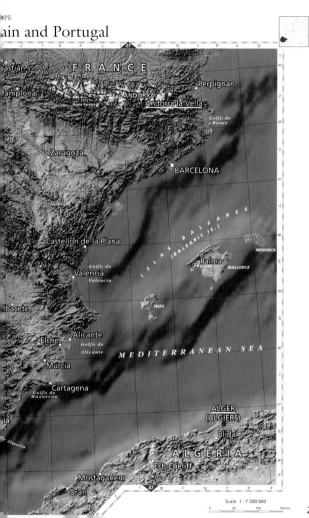

F R A N C E

Perpignan

ANDORRA
Monte Perdido 3355
Andorra la Vella

Golfo de
Rosas

Pamplona

astián

Zaragoza

BARCELONA

Castellón de la Plana

I S L A S   B A L E A R E S
(BALEARIC IS.)

MENORCA

Palma

MALLORCA

Golfo de
Valencia
Valencia

IBIZA

Ibacete

Elche

Alicante
Golfo de
Alicante

Murcia

M E D I T E R R A N E A N   S E A

Cartagena

Golfo de
Mazarron

ia

ALGER
(ALGIERS)

Blida

Almeri

A L G E R I A

Ech Cheliff

Mostaganem

Oran

Scale 1 : 7 500 000

0        50        100        150 km

Scale 1 : 5 625 000

0    50    100    150 km

31

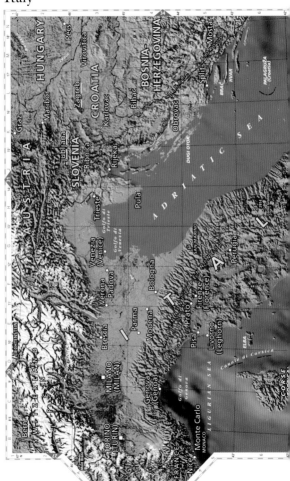

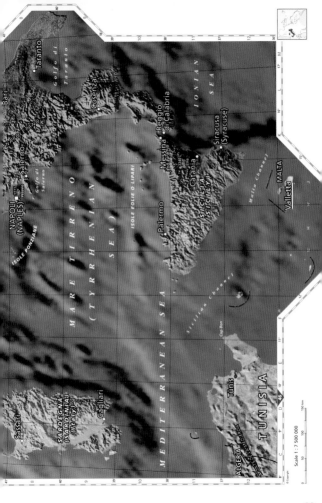

Taranto
Golfo di Taranto
Bari

Cosenza

Reggio di Calabria
Messina
IONIAN SEA
Catania
SICILIA
(SICILY)
Siracusa (Syracuse)

NAPOLI (NAPLES)
Salerno
Golfo di Salerno
ISOLE PONZIANE

MARE TIRRENO
(TYRRHENIAN SEA)
ISOLE EOLIE O LIPARI
Palermo

Malta Channel
MALTA
Valletta

Sicilian Channel
Cap Bon

MEDITERRANEAN SEA

SARDEGNA (SARDINIA) (Italy)
Sassari
Cagliari

TUNISIA
Tunis

ALGERIA

Scale 1 : 7 500 000

0    50    100    150 km

© Copyright

33

# The Balkans

Scale 1 : 7 500 000

0    50    100    150 km

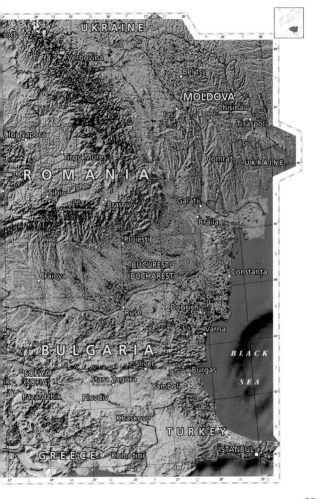

# Greece and West Turkey

Scale 1 : 7 500 000

0    50    100    150    200 km

ROMANIA
BUCUREŞTI
(BUCHAREST)
Constanţa
Simferopol' UKRAINE
Ruse
Sevastopol'
Varna
BULGARIA
STARA PLANINA
BLACK SEA
Burgas

İSTANBUL
MARMARA DENIZI
(SEA OF MARMARA)
İzmit
Karadeniz Boğazı
(Bosporus)
LESVOS
(LESBOS)
Bursa
KÖROĞLU DAĞLARI
Eskişehir
ANKARA
Kırıkkale
Sıv
T U
İZMIR
(SMYRNA)
Kayseri
3917
Erciyaş Dağı
Denizli
Konya
Kahraman
Antalya
TOROS DAĞLARI
Adana
Gaz
GREECE
RÓDHOS
(RHODES)
H
A

CYPRUS
Levkósia
(Nicosia)
Hamäh
1951
Mt Troodos
(Olympus)
Tráblous
(Tripoli)
LEBANON
DIMA
BEYROUTH
(BEIRUT)
(DAM
MEDITERRANEAN
SEA

© Copyright

Scale 1 : 12 500 000
0      100      200      300 km

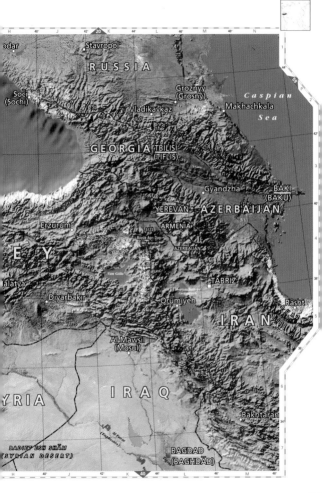

39

# Middle East

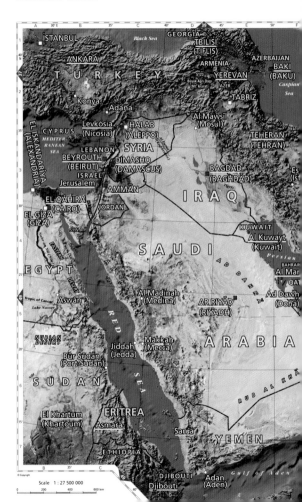

Scale 1 : 27 500 000

0    200    400    600 km

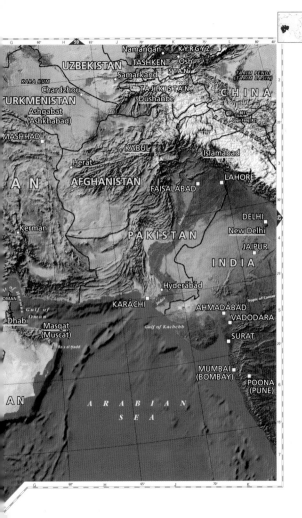

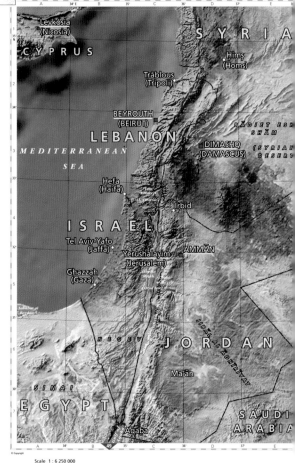

Scale 1 : 6 250 000

0    50    100    150 km

Maşqaţ (Muscat)

Gulf of Oman

OMAN

Bandar-e 'Abbās

Kermān

Sarīdābād

I R A N

Lār

Bandar-e Lengeh

Ash Shāriqah (Sharjah)

Dubayy (Dubai)

Shīrāz

Fīrūzābād

Deyyer

UNITED ARAB EMIRATES

Būshehr

Abū Zabī (Abu Dhabi)

BAHRAIN Al Manāmah (Manama)

QATAR Ad Dawḩah (Doha)

Ahvāz

Persian Gulf

Ad Dammām

AL ḤASĀ'

Al Başrah (Basra)

Ābādān

KUWAIT Al Kuwayt (Kuwait)

I R A Q

S A U D I

AD DAHNĀ'

AR RIYĀḌ (RIYADH)

A R A B I A

Scale 1 : 12 500 000

0    100    200    300 km

# Africa

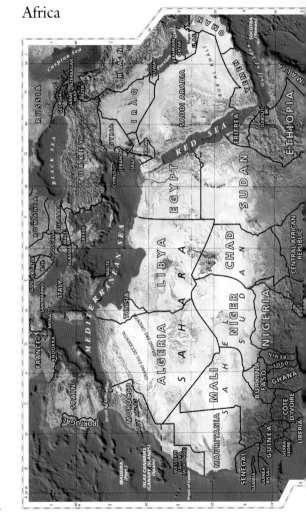

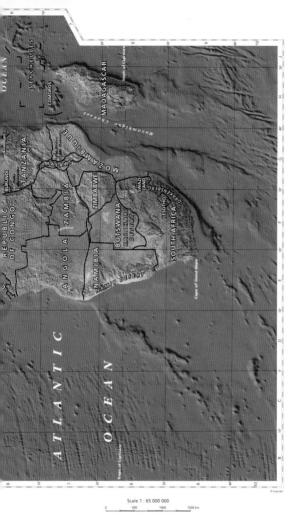

Scale 1 : 65 000 000

AÇORES
(AZORES)
(Port.)

MADEIRA
(Port.)

Strait of Gi

Tanger
(Tangier)

DĀR-EL-BEIDĀ □ Rabat
(CASABLANCA)

MOROCC

4165
Jebel Toubkal

HAUT ATL

ANTI ATLAS

Agadir

ISLAS CANARIAS
(CANARY ISLANDS)
(Spain)

Las Palmas

Es Semara

°Tindouf

*ATLANTIC*

Tropic of Cancer

Ad Dakhla

*OCEAN*

WESTERN SAHARA
(MOROCCO)

S

A

°Zouérat

Nouâdhibou

Atâr

°Taoud

Nouakchott

MAURITANIA

M A

DAKAR

'Ayoûn el Atroûs

Tombou

SENEGAL

S

A

Niger

Banjul

GAMBIA

H

U

Bissau

GUINEA-
BISSAU

ORANGO

GUINEA

Bamako

BURKIN

Ouagado

Bobo
Dioulasso

FAS

Conakry

Kankan

© Copyright

Scale 1 : 25 000 000

0    200    400    800 km

ALGER
(ALGIERS)
Oran
Cap
Bengut
Annaba
Constantine
Tunis
Palermo
*ITALY*
*SICILIA*
*(SICILY)*

*MEDITERRANEAN*

MALTA

*SEA*

Djelfa
Gabes
Sfax

*SAHARA ATLAS*

TUNISIA
Tarābulus
(Tripoli)
Mişrātah
Surt (Sirte)

Abbès
El Goléa
*GRAND ERG OCCIDENTAL*
*GRAND ERG ORIENTAL*

*L G E R I A*
*L I B Y A*

gane
AL HARŪJ
AL ASWAD

*A R A*
*F E Z Z*

Djanet

Tropic of Cancer

Madama

*TIBESTI*

I-n-Guezzam

*AÏR (AZBINE)*

*T É N É R É*

*N I G E R*
Agadez
*GRAND ERG DE BILMA*
Faya

*BODÉLÉ*

*A N*

*CHAD*

amey

Sokoto
Katsina
*NIGERIA*

# Northeast Africa

Scale 1 : 25 000 000

0    200    400    600 km

49

MAURITANIA

°Ayoûn el Atroûs

Tomboucto
*Niger*

DAKAR
SENEGAL

M A L I

Banjul
GAMBIA

BURKI
Ouagadou
FASO
Bobo Dioulasso

Bissau GUINEA-
BISSAU

ORANGO
G U I N E A

Bamako

Bolgatanga

*ORANGO*

Kankan

Odienné

Tar

Conakry
SIERRA
LEONE
Freetown
Bo

Nzérékoré

CÔTE
D'IVOIRE
Yamoussoukro

Bouaké
GHAN

Kumasi

Monrovia
River Cess

LIBERIA

ABIDJAN

Secondi-
Takoradi

Equator

A T L A N T I C

O C E A N

A
CAPE VERDE
*SÃO TIAGO*
Praia

O
15° N

B
1

2

© Copyright

Scale 1 : 25 000 000

0       200      400      600 km

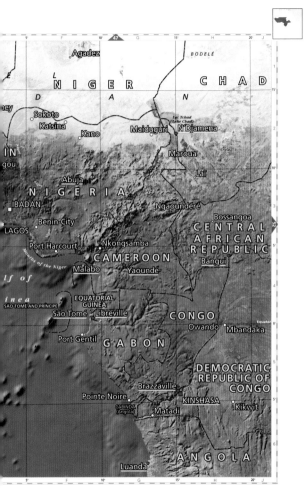

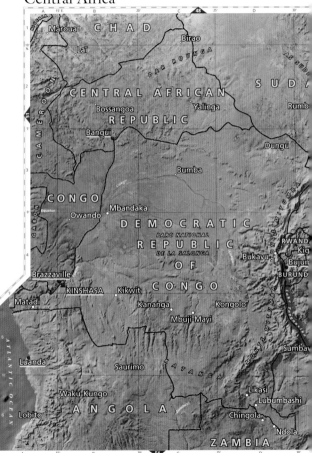

Scale 1 : 25 000 000

0    200    400    600 km

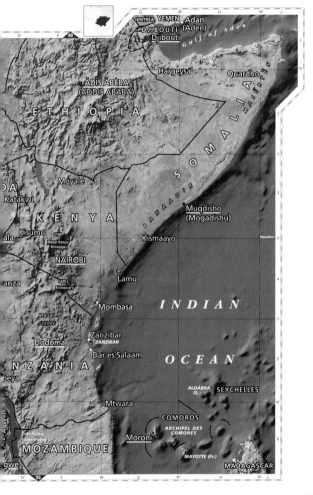

# Southern Africa

Saurimo

DEMOCRATIC
REPUBLIC
OF CONGO

Likasi

Lubum

Waku-Kungo

Chingola

Lobito

Nd

**A N G O L A**

Kab

**Z A M B I A**

Namibe

Lus

Livingstone

**ZIM**

Rundu

Bula

**N A M I B I A**

Francistown

**B O T S W A N A**

Tropic of Capricorn

Windhoek

Gaborone

*K A L A H A R I*
*D E S E R T*

Pret

**JOHANNESBUF**

Lüderitz

*Orange*
*Oranje*

Bloemfontein

Maseru
**LESOTHO**

**S O U T H   A F R I C A**

*A T L A N T I C*

*O C E A N*

St.
Helena
Bay

**CAPE TOWN**

East Lor

Port Elizabeth

*Cape of Good Hope*

*Cape Agulhas*

Scale 1 : 25 000 000

0    200    400    600 km

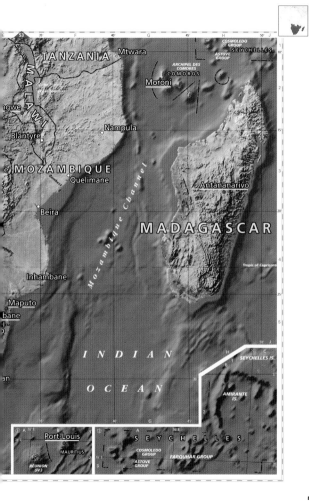

TANZANIA  Mtwara

ARCHIPEL DES COMOROS
COMORS

Moroni

COSMOLEDO GROUP
ASTOVE GROUP
SEYCHELLES

Nampula

MOZAMBIQUE

Quelimane

Antananarivo

Beira

MADAGASCAR

Blantyre

MALAWI

ngwe

Mozambique Channel

Inhambane

Tropic of Capricorn

Maputo
bane

INDIAN

OCEAN

an

SEYCHELLES IS.

AMIRANTE IS.

Port-Louis

MAURITIUS

RÉUNION
(Fr.)

SEYCHELLES

COSMOLEDO GROUP
ASTOVE GROUP

FARQUHAR GROUP

# Asia

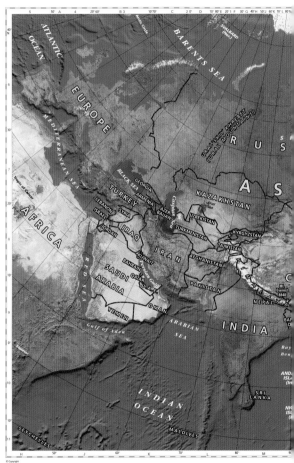

Equatorial Scale 1 : 71 250 000

0   400   800   1200   1600 km

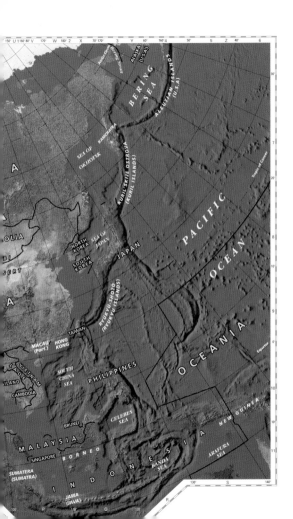

# Northwest Asia

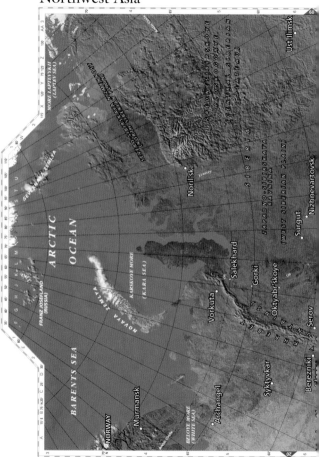

ARCTIC OCEAN

FRANZ JOSEFLAND (RUSSIA)

BARENTS SEA

NORWAY

Murmansk

Ardhangel

BELOYE MORE (WHITE SEA)

KARSKOYE MORE (KARA SEA)

NOVAYA ZEMLYA

SEVERNAYA ZEMLYA

MORE LAPTEVYKH (LAPTEV SEA)

SREDNESIBIRSKOYE PLOSKOGORYE (CENTRAL SIBERIAN PLATEAU)

SIBERIA

ZAPADNO-SIBIRSKAYA RAVNINA (WEST SIBERIAN PLAIN)

URAL KHREBET

Ust-Ilimsk

Norilsk

Yenisey

Nizhnevartovsk

Surgut

Salekhard

Gorki

Oktyabr'skoye

Serov

Vorkuta

Syktyvkar

Berezniki

© Copyright

58

Scale 1 : 30 000 000

0      200      400      600 km

59

# Northeast Asia

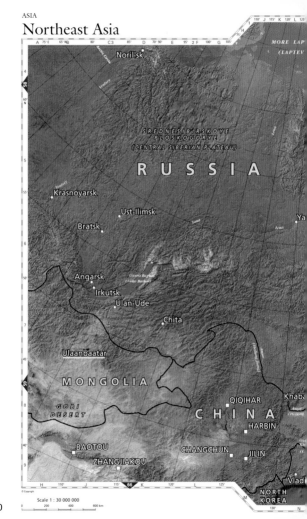

MORE LAP
(LAPTEV

RUSSIA

SREDNESIBIRSKOYE
PLOSKOGORYE
(CENTRAL SIBERIAN PLATEAU)

Noril'sk

Krasnoyarsk

Ust-Ilimsk

Bratsk

Angarsk

Irkutsk

Ulan-Ude

Ozero Baykal
(Lake Baikal)

Chita

Ya

Ulaanbaatar

MONGOLIA

GOBI
DESERT

Khaba

QIQIHAR

CHINA

HARBIN

BAOTOU

CHANGCHUN

JILIN

ZHANGJIAKOU

Vlad

NORTH
KOREA

Scale 1 : 30 000 000

0     200     400     600 km

60

RSKIYE OSTROVA

ERIAN ISLANDS)

*VOSTOČNO-SIBIRSKOYE MORE*
*(EAST SIBERIAN SEA)*

Lavrentiya

**ALASKA**
**(U.S.A.)**

*B E R I N G*

*S E A*

ALEUTIAN IS.
(U.S.A.)

Magadan

*H O K - K A I*

*(SEA OF OKHOTSK)*

Petropavlovsk-
Kamchatskiy

OSTROVA
SAKHALIN

nsomol'sk-
Amure

*PACIFIC*

Yuzhno Sakhalinsk.

*La Pérouse Strait*

*OCEAN*

Asahikawa

SAPPORO

*E /*

*- KAI*

HOKKAIDO

JAPAN

61

# Southern Asia

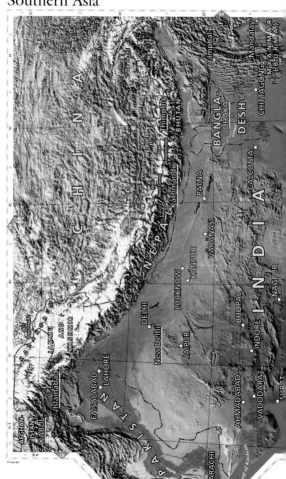

MYANMAR
(BURMA)

Mandalay

Imphal

CHITTAGONG

BANGLA-
DHAKA
DESH

CALCUTTA

Thimphu
BHUTAN

PATNA

Kathmandu

NEPAL

VARANASI

I N D I A

LUCKNOW

KANPUR

NAGPUR

C H I N A

DELHI

BHOPAL

New Delhi

JAIPUR

INDORE

JAMMU
AND
KASHMIR

LAHORE

VADODARA

AHMADABAD

FAISALABAD

AFGHAN-
ISTAN

Islamabad

KABUL

P A K I S T A N

SURAT

KARACHI

Gulf of Kutch

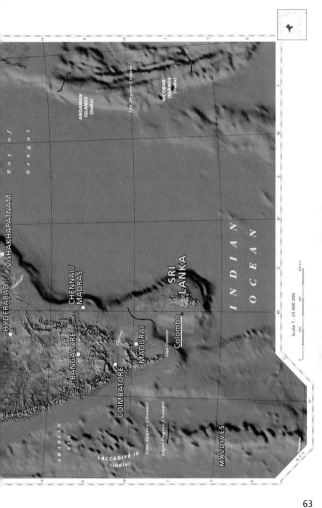

ANDAMAN
ISLANDS
(India)

Ten Degree Channel

NICOBAR
ISLANDS
(India)

B a y    o f

B e n g a l

HYDERABAD    VISHAKHAPATNAM

CHENNAI/
MADRAS

SRI
LANKA

I N D I A N

O C E A N

BANGALORE

Cape Comorin

COIMBATORE

MADURAI

Colombo

S A H Y A D R I    W E S T E R N    G H A T S

E A S T E R N    G H A T S

A R A B I A N

S E A

LACCADIVE IS.
(India)

Nine Degree Channel

Eight Degree Channel

MALDIVES

Equator

Scale 1 : 25 000 000

0    200    400    600 km

63

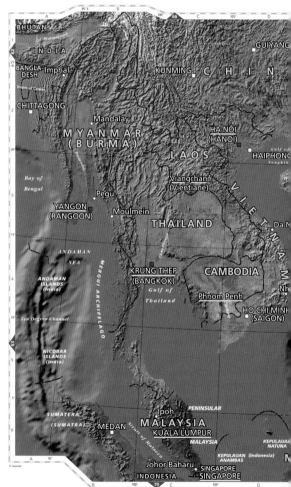

BHUTAN

INDIA

BANGLA-DESH

Imphal

CHITTAGONG

KUNMING

C H I N A

GUIYANG

Mandalay

MYANMAR (BURMA)

HA NOI (HANOI)

HAIPHONG

*Gulf of*

*Tongkin*

LAOS

*Bay of Bengal*

Pegu

Viangchan (Vientiane)

YANGON (RANGOON)

Moulmein

V I E T N A M

Da N

THAILAND

*ANDAMAN SEA*

KRUNG THEP (BANGKOK)

CAMBODIA

Nh

ANDAMAN ISLANDS (India)

*MERGUI ARCHIPELAGO*

*Gulf of Thailand*

Phnom Penh

*Ten Degree Channel*

HO CHI MINH (SAIGON)

NICOBAR ISLANDS (India)

SUMATERA (SUMATRA)

PENINSULAR

Ipoh

MALAYSIA

MEDAN

*Strait of Malacca*

KUALA LUMPUR

MALAYSIA

KEPULAUAN ANAMBAS

KEPULAUAN (Indonesia) NATUNA

N

Johor Baharu

SINGAPORE

SINGAPORE

INDONESIA

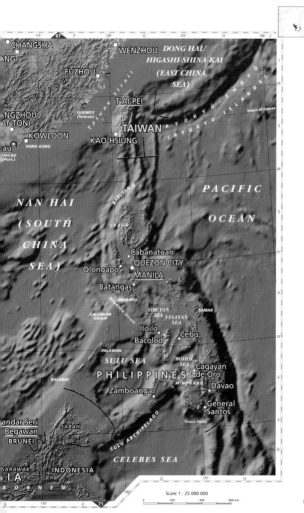

CHANGSHA

WENZHOU

DONG HAI/
HIGASHI-SHINA-KAI
(EAST CHINA
SEA)

FUZHOU

NGZHOU
ANTON)

QUEMOY
(Taiwan)

T'AI-PEI

TAIWAN

KOWLOON

KAO-HSIUNG

Tropic of Cancer

HONG KONG

au
ACAU
(Port.)

NAN HAI

(SOUTH

CHINA

SEA)

BABUYAN IS.

LUZON

PACIFIC

OCEAN

Cabanatuan

QUEZON CITY

Olongapo

MANILA

Batangas

MINDORO

MINDORO Strait

CALAMIAN
GROUP

SIBUYAN
SEA

VISAYAN
SEA

SAMAR

Iloilo

Bacolod

Cebu

PALAWAN

BOHOL
SEA

SULU SEA

PHILIPPINES

Cagayan
de Oro

BALABAC

MINDANAO

Davao

Zamboanga

General
Santos

andar Seri
Begawan

BRUNEI

SABAH

Tinaca Point

SULU ARCHIPELAGO

SARAWAK

INDONESIA

I A

CELEBES SEA

B O R N E O

Scale 1 : 25 000 000

0      200      400      600 km

65

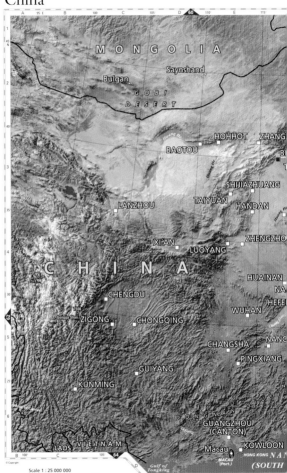

MONGOLIA

Saynshand

Bulgan

G O B I
D E S E R T

HOHHOT    ZHANG

BAOTOU

SHIJIAZHUANG

LANZHOU    TAIYUAN    HANDAN

C H I N A    XI'AN    LOUYANG    ZHENGZHO

HUAINAN
NA
HEFE
CHENGDU    WUHAN

Gongga Shan    ZIGONG    CHONGQING

CHANGSHA    NANC

PINGXIANG

GUIYANG

KUNMING

D O N G N A N

GUANGZHOU
(CANTON)

LAOS    V I E T N A M    Macau    KOWLOON

MACAU    HONG KONG    NA
(Port.)

(SOUTH

Gulf of
Tongking

© Copyright

Scale 1 : 25 000 000

0    200    400    600 km

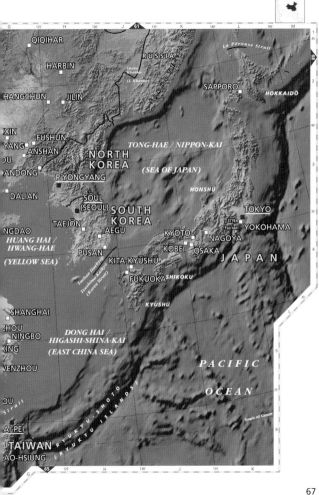

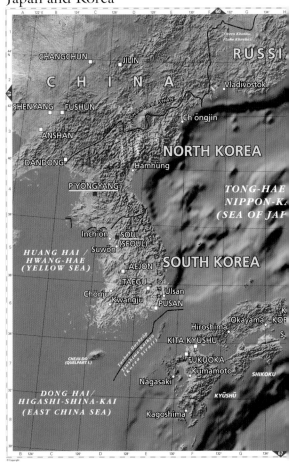

ASIA

Japan and Korea

CHANGCHUN
JILIN
RUSSIA
*Ozero Khanka*
*(Lake Khanka)*

C H I N A
Vladivostok

SHENYANG FUSHUN
Ch'ŏngjin
*CHANGBAI SHAN*

ANSHAN
NORTH KOREA

DANDONG
Hamhŭng
*TONG-HAE*
*NIPPON-KA*
*(SEA OF JAP*

P'YŎNGYANG

Inch'ŏn SŎUL
(SEOUL)
SOUTH KOREA

Suwŏn

*HUANG HAI /*
*HWANG-HAE*
*(YELLOW SEA)*
TAEJŎN

TAEGU
Chŏnju Ulsan
Kwangju
PUSAN

Okayama K
KOB
Hiroshima S.

CHEJU-DO
(QUELPART I.)
KITA-KYŪSHŪ
*Tsushima Strait*
*(Korea Strait)*
FUKUOKA
SHIKOKU
Kumamoto
Nagasaki
KYŪSHŪ

*DONG HAI /*
*HIGASHI-SHINA-KAI*
*(EAST CHINA SEA)*

Kagoshima

© Copyright

Scale 1 : 12 500 000
0    100    200    300 km

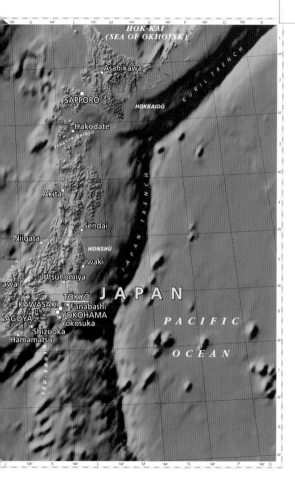

138° K 140° L 142° M 144° N 146° P 148° Q 150° R

HOK-KAI
(SEA OF OKHOTSK)

Asahikawa

SAPPORO

HOKKAIDŌ

KURIL TRENCH

Hakodate

Tsugaru-kaikyo

JAPAN TRENCH

Akita

Sendai

Niigata

HONSHŪ

Iwaki

awa  Utsunomiya

JAPAN

KAWASAKI  TŌKYŌ  Funabashi
NAGOYA  YOKOHAMA
Yokosuka
Shizuoka
Hamamatsu

PACIFIC

OCEAN

IZU SHOTŌ

J 138° K 140° L 142° M 144° N 146° P 148° Q

Scale 1 : 25 000 000

0    200    400    600 km

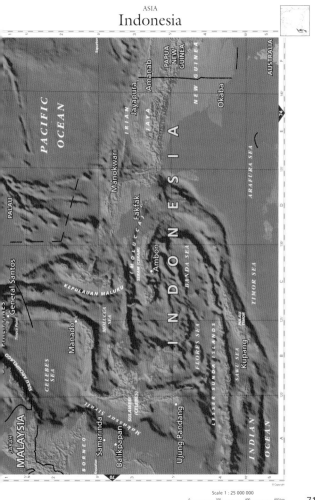

Scale 1 : 25 000 000

0    200    400    600    800 km

# Oceania

Scale 1 : 87 500 000

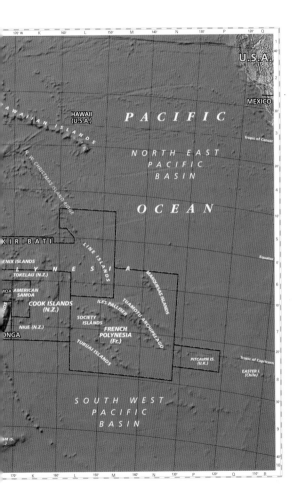

U.S.A.

MEXICO

HAWAII
(U.S.A.)

PACIFIC

NORTH EAST
PACIFIC
BASIN

Tropic of Cancer

HAWAIIAN ISLANDS

N.W. CHRISTMAS ISLAND RIDGE

OCEAN

KIRIBATI

LINE ISLANDS

Equator

PHOENIX ISLANDS

TOKELAU (N.Z.)

P O L Y N E S I A

MARQUESAS ISLANDS

AMOA  AMERICAN
SAMOA

COOK ISLANDS
(N.Z.)

ILES PALLISER

TUAMOTU ARCHIPELAGO

SOCIETY
ISLANDS

NIUE (N.Z.)

FRENCH
POLYNESIA
(Fr.)

ONGA

TUBUAI ISLANDS

PITCAIRN IS.
(U.K.)

Tropic of Capricorn

EASTER I.
(Chile)

SOUTH WEST
PACIFIC
BASIN

M IS.

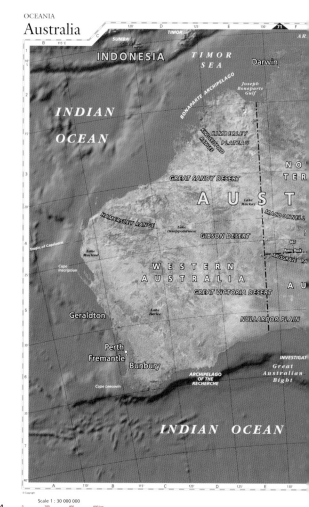

INDONESIA

SUMBA

TIMOR

AR

TIMOR SEA

Darwin

INDIAN

OCEAN

Bonaparte Archipelago

Joseph
Bonaparte
Gulf

KIMBERLEY
PLATEAU

KING LEOPOLD
RANGES

GREAT SANDY DESERT

NO
TER

AUST

Lake
Mackay

MACDONNELL

HAMERSLEY RANGE

Lake
Disappointment

GIBSON DESERT

Tropic of Capricorn

Lake
Macleod

867
Ayers Rock
MUSGRAVE RA

Cape
Inscription

WESTERN
AUSTRALIA

GREAT VICTORIA DESERT

AU

Geraldton

Lake
Barlee

NULLARBOR PLAIN

Perth
Fremantle

Bunbury

ARCHIPELAGO
OF THE
RECHERCHE

INVESTIGAT

Great
Australian
Bight

Cape Leeuwin

INDIAN OCEAN

74

Scale 1 : 30 000 000

0    200    400    600 km

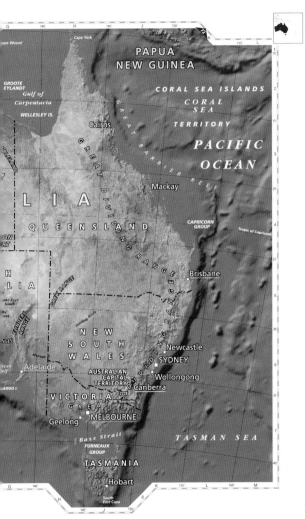

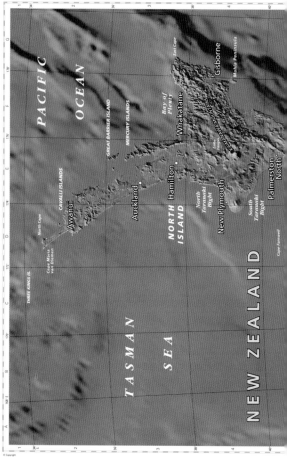

Scale 1 : 10 000 000

0    100    200 km

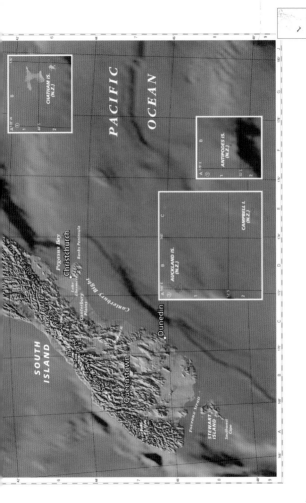

PACIFIC OCEAN

CHATHAM IS.
(N.Z.)

ANTIPODES IS.
(N.Z.)

AUCKLAND IS.
(N.Z.)

CAMPBELL I.
(N.Z.)

SOUTH ISLAND

Christchurch

Pegasus Bay

Banks Peninsula

Lake Ellesmere

Canterbury Plains

Canterbury Bight

Dunedin

Queenstown

STEWART ISLAND

Foveaux Strait

Southwest Cape

# North America

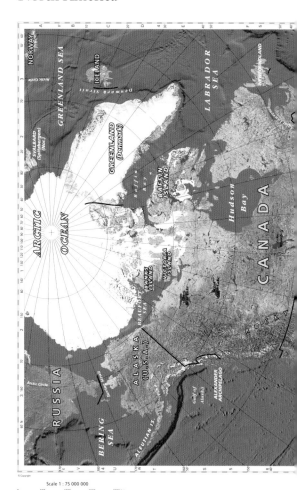

Scale 1 : 75 000 000

0   500   1000   1500   2000 km

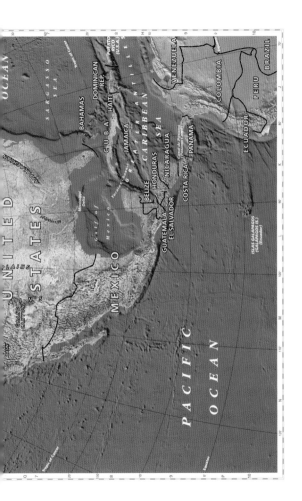

Scale 1 : 30 000 000

0    200    400    600 km

Baffin Bay

GREENLAND
(Denmark)

BAFFIN
ISLAND

Godthab

Davis Strait

Denmark Strait

Arctic Circle

LABRADOR SEA

Hudson Strait

NEWFOUNDLAND AND LABRADOR

A

Hudson Bay

BELCHER
ISLANDS

NEWFOUNDLAND

St. John's

ONTARIO

QUÉBEC

Gulf of
St. Lawrence

ST. PIERRE
ET MIQUELON (Fr.)

P.E.I. Charlotte-
town

NEW
BRUNSWICK

Québec

Fredericton    Halifax

NOVA
SCOTIA

Lake
Superior

MAINE

A.

Montpelier

VER-
MONT
NEW
HAMP-
SHIRE

Ottawa

MONTRÉAL

Augusta

Gulf of
Maine

ATLANTIC

MICHIGAN

TORONTO

Lake Ontario

Niagara Falls

NEW
YORK

Concord

MASS.

OCEAN

Cape Cod

Lake
Huron

MILWAUKEE

BUFFALO

Albany

Hartford

BOSTON

PROVIDENCE

RHODE I.

DETROIT

PENNSYLVANIA

NEW YORK

N.J.

81

# United States of America

© Copyright

Scale 1 : 33 500 000

0    200    400    600    800 km

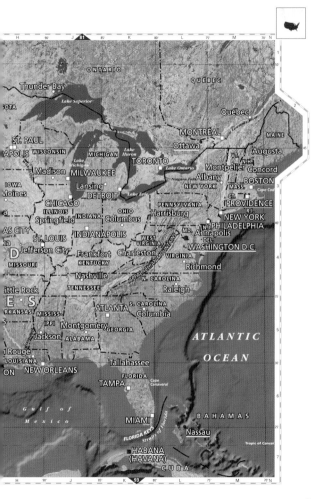

# United States, Northwest

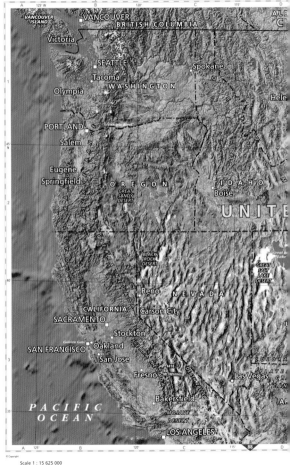

Scale 1 : 15 625 000

0    100    200    300 km

SASKATCHEWAN
MANITOBA

A   D   A

NORTH DAKOTA

N T A N A
Bismarck        Fargo

G R E A T

D R I F T   P R A I R I E S

Pierre
SOUTH DAKOTA

P L A I N S

WYOMING
TATES

NEBRASKA

Cheyenne

Omaha

Platte River
Lincoln

DENVER

Colorado
Springs        KANSAS
COLORADO
Pueblo
Arkansas River        Topeka

GREAT PRAIRIES

Wichita

NEW MEXICO
Santa Fe
Tulsa

Alberquerque
Amarillo        Oklahoma City
TEXAS        OKLAHOMA

# United States, Northeast

MANITOBA

ONTARIO

Thunder Bay

N. DAK.

Fargo

Duluth

*Lake Superior*

MINNESOTA

ST. PAUL

MINNEAPOLIS

WISCONSIN

*Lake Michigan*

S. DAK.

Madison

MILWAUKEE

Flint

MICHIGAN

IOWA

Rockford

Lansing

DETROIT

Cedar Rapids

CHICAGO

Omaha

Des Moines

Davenport

Fort Wayne

OH

Lincoln

Peoria

INDIANA

NEBR.

ILLINOIS

Springfield

INDIANAPOLIS

Co

UNITED STATES

KANSAS CITY

ST. LOUIS

CINCINN

Topeka

Jefferson City

Louisville

Frankfort

KANSAS

MISSOURI

Evansville

Lexingt

Springfield

KENTUCKY

Tulsa

ARKANSAS

Nashville

TENNESSEE

Chattanoog

OKLAHOMA

Little Rock

Memphis

MISSIS-

Huntsville

SIPPI

ALABAMA

GEORGIA

© Copyright

Scale 1 : 15 625 000

0    100    200    300 km

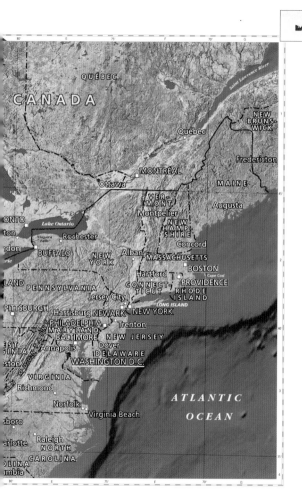

QUÉBEC

CANADA

Saint Lawrence River

Québec

NEW BRUNSWICK

MONTRÉAL

Fredericton

Ottawa

MAINE

VER-
MONT

Augusta

Montpelier

NEW
HAMP-
SHIRE

Concord

ONTO

Lake Ontario

ton

Rochester

Niagara Falls

ndon

Albany

MASSACHUSETTS

erie

BUFFALO

NEW
YORK

BOSTON

Hartford

PROVIDENCE

LAND

PENNSYLVANIA

CONNECT-
ICUT

RHODE
ISLAND

Jersey City

LONG ISLAND

PITTSBURGH

Harrisburg NEWARK

NEW YORK

PHILADELPHIA
MARYLAND

Trenton

EST
INIA

BALTIMORE

NEW JERSEY

Dover

eston

Annapolis

DELAWARE

WASHINGTON D.C.

VIRGINIA

Richmond

sboro

Norfolk

Virginia Beach

ATLANTIC

OCEAN

arlotte

Raleigh

NORTH
CAROLINA

OLINA

mbia

Scale 1 : 15 625 000
0    100    200    300 km

E · 105° · 35 · F · 100° · G · 40°

DENVER

COLORADO

Colorado
Springs

Topeka

KANSAS

Pueblo · Arkansas R. · Wichita

GREAT PRAIRIES

Arkansas R.

1

A B O
A U

Santa Fe

Albuquerque

Amarillo

Tulsa
Oklahoma City

OKLAHOMA

NEW MEXICO

UNITED STATES · Wichita Falls

Lubbock

Fort Worth

DALLAS

2

El Paso

Ciudad
Juárez

TEXAS

Austin

SAN
ANTONIO

Chihuahua

Rio Grande

SIERRA MADRE ORIENTAL

MEXICO

Corpus Christi

3

SIERRA MADRE OCCIDENTAL

Torreón

MONTERREY

Río Bravo del Norte

Tropic of Cancer

San Luis
Potosí

92

157° · 156° · 155° · 105° · F · 100° · G

E · 156° · 157°

HAWAII

(U.S.A.)

lu

Kauai Channel

Kaiwi Channel

4205
Mauna
Kea

Hilo

HAWAII

Ka Lae

89

# United States, Southeast

Scale 1 : 15 625 000

0 100 200 300 km

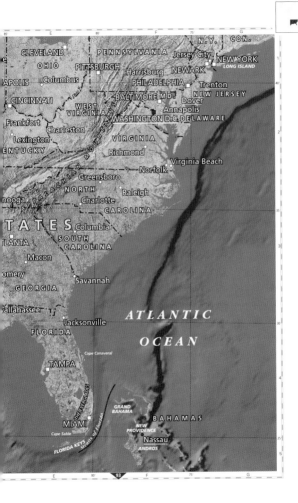

# Central America and the Caribbean

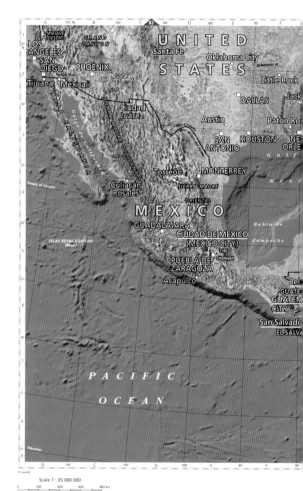

Scale 1 : 35 000 000
0   200   400   600   800 km

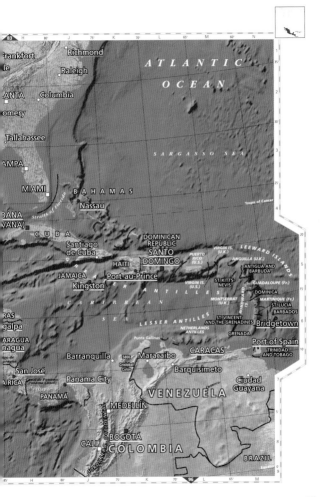

Frankfort
le
Richmond
Raleigh
ANTA
Columbia
omery
Tallahassee
AMPA
MIAMI
BAHAMAS
Nassau
BANA
VANA)
Straits of Florida
C U B A
Santiago
de Cuba
DOMINICAN
REPUBLIC
SANTO
DOMINGO
VIRGIN IS.
(U.K.)
LEEWARD ISLANDS
PUERTO
RICO
(U.S.)
ANGUILLA (U.K.)
HAITI
Port-au-Prince
JAMAICA
Kingston
VIRGIN IS.
(U.S.)
ST.KITTS-
NEVIS
ANTIGUA AND
BARBUDA
GUADALOUPE (Fr.)
DOMINICA
ANTILLES
MONTSERRAT
MARTINIQUE (Fr.)
ST.LUCIA
BARBADOS
C A R I B B E A N
S E A
LESSER ANTILLES
NETHERLANDS
ANTILLES
Punta Gallinas
ST.VINCENT
AND THE GRENADINES
GRENADA
Bridgetown
Port of Spain
RAS
galpa
ARAGUA
nagua
go de
rragosa
San José
RICA
Barranquilla
5800
Cristóbal
Colón
Maracaibo
CARACAS
Barquisimeto
TRINIDAD
AND TOBAGO
Panama City
VENEZUELA
Ciudad
Guayana
PANAMÁ
Canal de Panama
(Panama Canal)
MEDELLÍN
CORDILLERA OCCIDENTAL
CALI
BOGOTÁ
COLOMBIA
BRAZIL

ATLANTIC
OCEAN
SARGASSO SEA
Tropic of Cancer

93

# South America

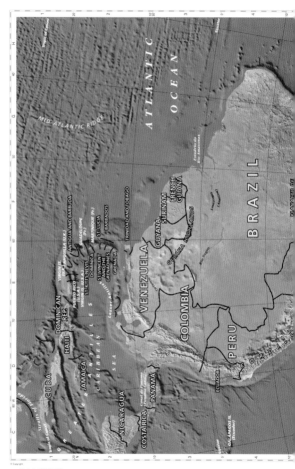

Scale 1 : 60 750 000

0   200   400   600   800   1000 km

© Copyright

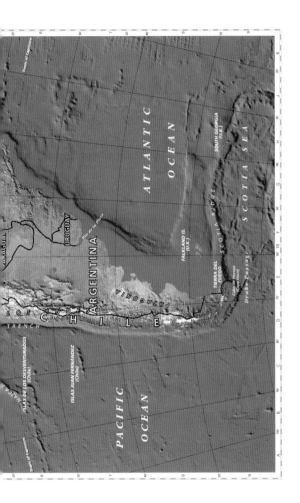

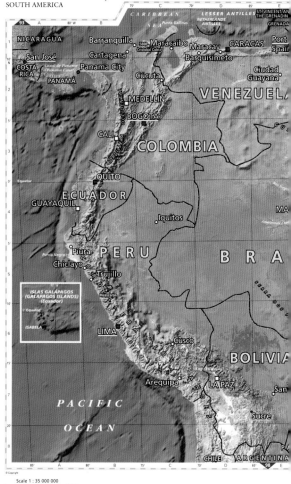

Scale 1 : 35 000 000

0    200    400    600 km

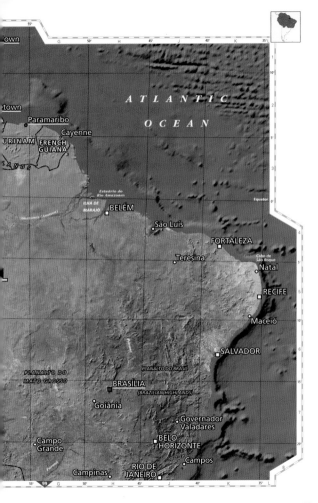

ATLANTIC

OCEAN

own

55°

G   50°   H   45°   J   40°   K   35° L

town

Paramaribo

Cayenne

URINAM   FRENCH
GUIANA

A N D S

Estuário do
Río Amazonas

ILHA DE
MARAJÓ   BELÉM

São Luís

FORTALEZA

Teresina   Cabo de
São Roque

Natal

RECIFE

Maceió

SALVADOR

Amazonas (Amazon)

Equator

PLANALTO DO
MATO GROSSO   PLANALTO DO BRASIL

BRASÍLIA
(BRAZILIAN HIGHLANDS)

Goiânia

Governador
Valadares

Campo
Grande   BELO
HORIZONTE

Campos

Campinas   RIO DE
JANEIRO

55°   99   G   50°   H   45°   J   40°   K   35° L

# South America, South

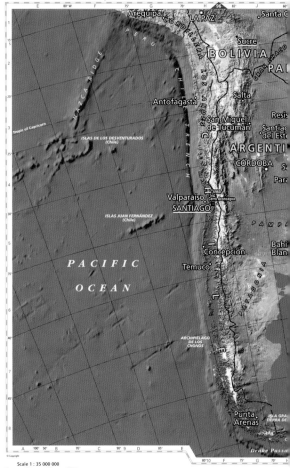

Scale 1 : 35 000 000

0    200    400    600 km

Campo
Grande

BELO
HORIZONTE

**B R A Z I L**

Campinas          • Campos

Santos   • SÃO PAULO     RIO DE JANEIRO

ción

□ CURITIBA

tes

• PORTO ALEGRE

**GUAY**

MONTEVIDEO

s

ar del Plata

*A T L A N T I C*

*O C E A N*

Tropic of Capricorn

ND IS.
K.)
Stanley

SOUTH GEORGIA
(U.K.)

SCOTIA RIDGE

*S C O T I A   S E A*

# Polar Regions

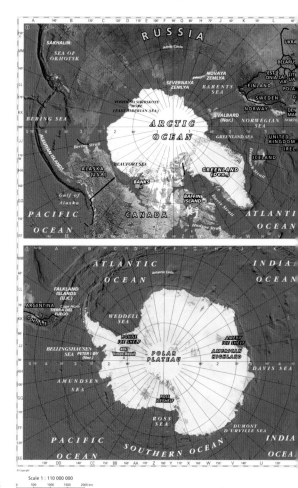

Scale 1 : 110 000 000

0    500    1000    1500    2000 km

# Global

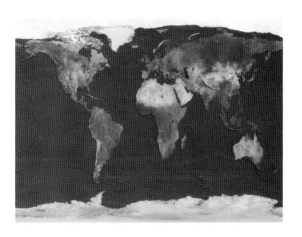

# Facts and Figures

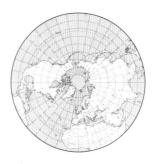

## Dimensions of the Earth

| | |
|---|---|
| Circumference of the Equator | 40,076 km |
| Total surface area of the Earth | 510,100,933 km$^2$ |
| Area of dry land (29.2%) | 149,408,563 km$^2$ |
| Area of sea (70.8%) | 360,692,370 km$^2$ |

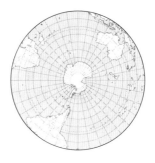

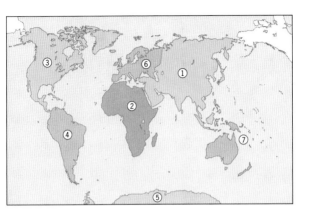

## Continental Land Surface

| | | |
|---|---|---|
| **1.** | Asia | 43,608,000 km$^2$ |
| **2.** | Africa | 30,335,000 km$^2$ |
| **3.** | North America | 25,349,000 km$^2$ |
| **4.** | South America | 17,611,000 km$^2$ |
| **5.** | Antarctica | 13,340,000 km$^2$ |
| **6.** | Europe | 10,498,000 km$^2$ |
| **7.** | Australia and Oceania | 8,923,000 km$^2$ |

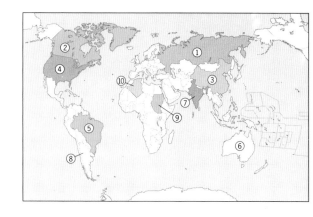

## Largest Countries according to area

| | | |
|---|---|---|
| **1.** | Russia | 17,100,000 km$^2$ |
| **2.** | Canada | 9,976,139 km$^2$ |
| **3.** | China | 9,572,980 km$^2$ |
| **4.** | United States | 9,363,166 km$^2$ |
| **5.** | Brazil | 8,511,996 km$^2$ |
| **6.** | Australia | 7,682,300 km$^2$ |
| **7.** | India | 3,166,829 km$^2$ |
| **8.** | Argentina | 2,780,092 km$^2$ |
| **9.** | Sudan | 2,505,813 km$^2$ |
| **10.** | Algeria | 2,381,740 km$^2$ |

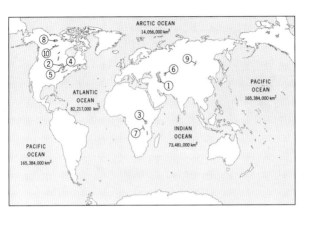

## Oceans and largest inland waters

| | | |
|---|---|---|
| **1.** | Caspian Sea (Salt) (Asia) | 371,000 km$^2$ |
| **2.** | Lake Superior (N. America) | 83,270 km$^2$ |
| **3.** | Lake Victoria (Africa) | 68,800 km$^2$ |
| **4.** | Lake Huron (N. America) | 60,700 km$^2$ |
| **5.** | Lake Michigan (N. America) | 58,020 km$^2$ |
| **6.** | Aral Sea (Salt) (Asia) | 36,000 km$^2$ |
| **7.** | Lake Tanganyika (Africa) | 32,900 km$^2$ |
| **8.** | Great Bear Lake (N. America) | 31,790 km$^2$ |
| **9.** | Lake Baikal (Asia) | 30,500 km$^2$ |
| **10.** | Great Slave Lake (N. America) | 28,440 km$^2$ |

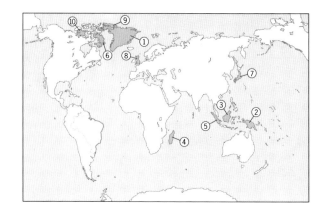

## Largest islands of the world

| | | |
|---|---|---|
| **1.** | Greenland | 2,175,600 km² |
| **2.** | New Guinea | 808,510 km² |
| **3.** | Borneo | 757,050 km² |
| **4.** | Madagascar | 594,180 km² |
| **5.** | Sumatra | 524,100 km² |
| **6.** | Baffin Island | 476,070 km² |
| **7.** | Honshu | 230,455 km² |
| **8.** | Great Britain | 229,870 km² |
| **9.** | Ellesmere Island | 212,690 km² |
| **10.** | Victoria Island | 212,200 km² |

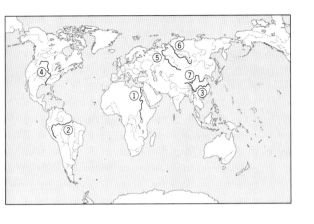

## Longest rivers of the world

| | | |
|---|---|---|
| **1.** | Nile (Africa) | 6,695 km |
| **2.** | Amazon (S. America) | 6,515 km |
| **3.** | Chang-Jiang/Yangtze (Asia) | 6,380 km |
| **4.** | Mississippi-Missouri (N. America) | 6,019 km |
| **5.** | Ob-Irtysh (Asia) | 5,570 km |
| **6.** | Jenisey-Angara (Asia) | 5,550 km |
| **7.** | Huang He-Yellow River (Asia) | 5,464 km |

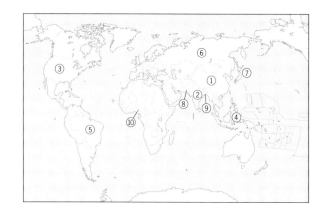

## Largest countries according to population

| 1. | China | 1,185,000,000 |
|---|---|---|
| 2. | India | 903,000,000 |
| 3. | United States | 257,000,000 |
| 4. | Indonesia | 188,000,000 |
| 5. | Brazil | 159,000,000 |
| 6. | Russia | 150,000,000 |
| 7. | o Japan | 124,900,000 |
| 8. | Pakistan | 122,400,000 |
| 9. | Bangladesh | 122,280,000 |
| 10. | Nigeria | 92,800,000 |

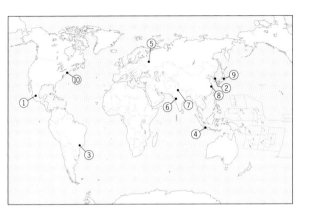

## Largest cities of the world

| | | |
|---|---|---|
| **1.** | Mexico City | 15,047,000 |
| **2.** | Seoul | 10,628,000 |
| **3.** | Sao Paulo | 9,480,427 |
| **4.** | Jakarta | 9,000,000 |
| **5.** | Moscow | 8,967,000 |
| **6.** | Bombay | 8,400,000 |
| **7.** | Delhi | 8,380,000 |
| **8.** | Shanghai | 8,214,436 |
| **9.** | Tokyo | 7,976,000 |
| **10.** | New York | 7,322,564 |

# Satellite
# Images
## — OF THE —
# World

A thirty-six page selection of
stunning satellite images featuring
major cities and contrasting
geographical habitats from around
the world.
These "zoomed in" images of earth
are breath-takingly detailed and
provide another perspective of our
natural and man-made world.

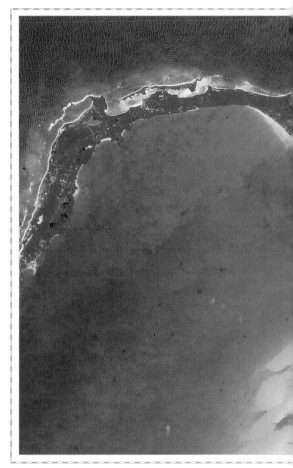

Eleuthera in the Bahamas where spectacular sandbanks
are visible under the water.

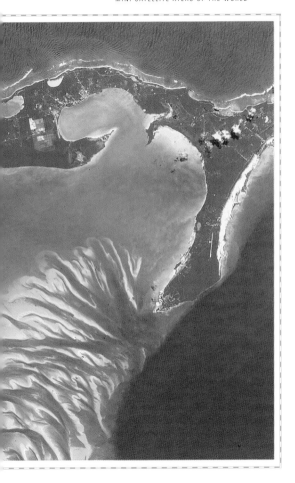

Part of the Paraná river of Brazil banked on either side
by a patchwork of cultivated land.

A view of the Exmouth peninsula in Chile where, from an altitude of 3000m, glaciers can be seen slowly edging into the Pacific Ocean.

Two worlds collide - the Sahara Desert in the top half of the picture
meets an Algerian mountain spur.

The mouth of the Guadalquivir River in Spain showing the development of a coastal spit and cultivated land in the low-lying, river flood plain.

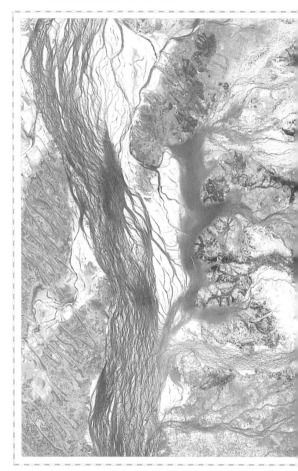

The incredible arteries of the Diamantina River during
the long dry Australian summer.

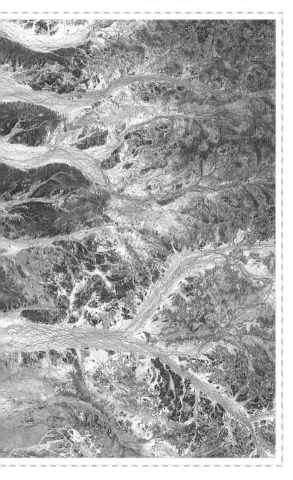

The Highlands and Islands of Scotland, where snow can clearly be seen
on the peaks to the right of the picture.

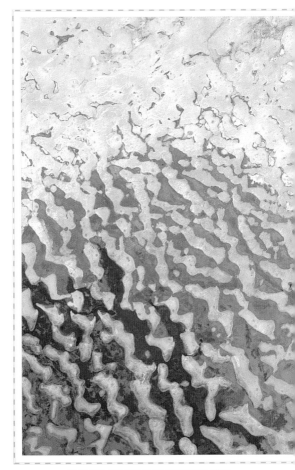

Dunes in the Sahara Desert show the powerful effect
of the wind, shaping the environment.

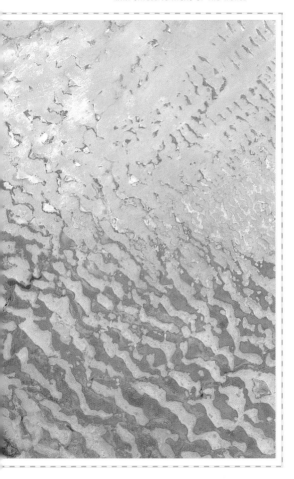

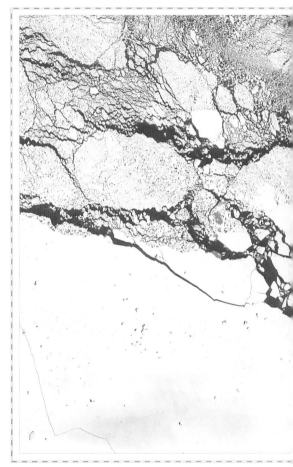

The edge of the Antarctic ice fields where the breaking
icebergs can be as large as 60km square.

The delta of the Mahakam River surrounded by dense forest near
Kalimantan, Borneo. Clouds at the top of the
picture cast shadows on the ground below.

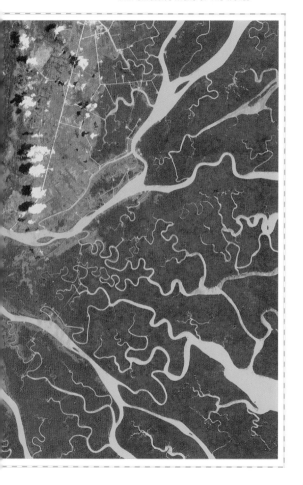

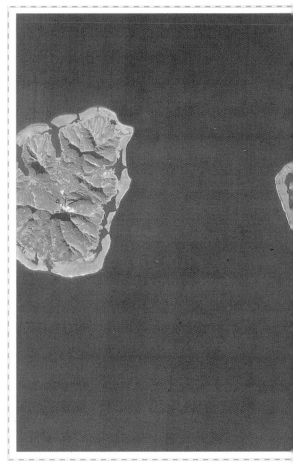

The amazing coral reefs that surround the islands of Tahiti on the right,
and Moorea on the left.

The city of Neuquén, Argentina between the Rio Negro and the Rio Neuquén.
Irrigation from the rivers allows land to be cultivated, shown here in red.
Lake Pellegrini is visible to the north.

The dramatic effect of rivers and erosion in the central Andes of Bolivia.

Isla Isabela, the largest of the volcanic islands of the Galapagos archipelago.

A volcanic landscape near Atacama in Chile. Below, a salt lake is clearly
visible against the mountain scenery. A river flows through
the valley floor from right to left of the image.

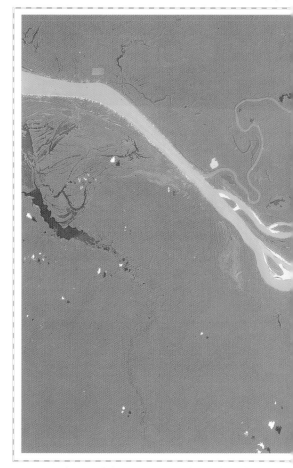

The Rio Grande de Santiago in Mexico, and its meandering tributaries.

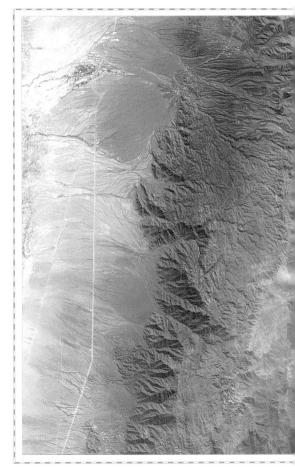

The eastern Andes near Catamarca in Argentina. Clearly visible
on the left is the straight line of a highway.

The Gibson Desert in Western Australia. An ever-changing aeolian landscape.

# Glossary

## A

| | | |
|---|---|---|
| abu | arabic | mountain |
| açude | portugese | reservoir |
| akra | greek | peninsula |
| alb | german | mountain, peak |
| alpen | german | mountains |
| alpes | french | mountains |
| alpi | italian | mountains |
| archipiélago | spanish | archipelago |

## B

| | | |
|---|---|---|
| bab | arabic | strait |
| bahia | spanish | bay |
| bahir, bahr | arabic | river, lake, bay |
| baie | french | bay |
| baja | spanish | lower |
| bandar | arabic, malay, persian, somalian | port, harbour |
| baraji | turkish | dam |
| ben | gaelic | mountain(s) |
| berg(e) | german | mountain(s) |
| bogazi | turkish | strait |
| bucht | german | bay |
| bulu | indonesian | mountain |

## C

| | | |
|---|---|---|
| cabo | spanish | cape |
| canal | english, french, spanish | canal, channel |
| canale | italian | canal, channel, strait |
| cerro | spanish | mountain |
| chett, chott | arabic | salt lake, marsh |
| chutes | french | waterfalls |
| co | tibetan | lake |
| collines | french | hills |
| cordillera | spanish | mountains |

## D

| | | |
|---|---|---|
| dag(i) | turkish | mountain |
| daglari) | turkish | mountains |
| danau | indonesian | lake |
| darja | persian | river |
| daryacheh | persian | lake |
| dasht | persian | desert |
| desierto | spanish | desert |
| djebel | arabic | mountain |

## E

| | | |
|---|---|---|
| embalse | spanish | reservoir |
| erg | arabic | desert with dunes |
| ezero | macedonian | lake |

## F

| | | |
|---|---|---|
| feng | chinese | peak |
| fjördur | icelandic | fjord |
| flói | icelandic | bay |

## G

| | | |
|---|---|---|
| gebirge | german | mountains |
| golfe | french | gulf, bay |
| golfo | italian, spanish | gulf, bay |
| gölü | turkish | lake |
| gora | russian | mountain |
| G., gunung | indonesian, malay | mountain |

## H

| | | |
|---|---|---|
| hai | chinese | lake, sea |
| hamun | persian | lake, marsh |
| hawr | arabic | lake |
| he | chinese | river |
| hory | czech | mountains |
| hu | chinese | lake |

## I

| | | |
|---|---|---|
| île(s) | french | island(s) |
| ilha(s) | portugese | island(s) |
| isla(s) | spanish | island(s) |

## J

| | | |
|---|---|---|
| jabal | arabic | mountain(s) |
| -järvi | finnish | lake |
| jaza'ir | arabic | islands |
| jazirat | arabic | island |
| jazireh | persian | island |
| jebel | arabic | mountain |
| jezioro | polish | lake |
| jiang | chinese | river |
| jibal | arabic | mountains |
| joki | finnish | river |
| jökull | icelandic | glacier |

## K

| | | |
|---|---|---|
| kepulauan | indonesian | islands |
| khrebet | russian | mountain range |
| kólpos | greek | gulf, bay |
| kryazh | russian | ridge |
| kuh | persian | mountain |
| kum | turkish | sandy desert |

## L

| | | |
|---|---|---|
| lac | french | lake |
| lacul | romanian | lake |
| lago | italian, spanish | lake |
| lagoa | portugese | lagoon |
| laguna | spanish | lake, lagoon |
| ligeni | albanian | lake |
| limni | greek | lake |
| ling | chinese | mountain range |
| loch, lough | gaelic | lake |

## M

| | | |
|---|---|---|
| mak | turkish | river |
| mar | spanish | sea |
| massif | french | mountains |
| meer | dutch | sea |
| monte | italian, spanish | mountain |
| mont(s) | french | mountain(s) |
| munti | romanian | mountains |

## N

| | | |
|---|---|---|
| nafud | arabic | desert |
| nevado | spanish | snow-capped mountain |
| nuruu | mongolian | mountains |
| nuur | mongolian | lake |

## O

| | | |
|---|---|---|
| óros | greek | mountain(s) |
| ostrov(a) | russian | island(s) |
| ozero | russian | lake |

## P

| | | |
|---|---|---|
| parc national | french | national pa... |
| pegunungan | indonesian, malay | mountain ran... |
| pendi | chinese | ba... |
| pic | french | pe... |
| pico | spanish | pe... |
| planalto | portugese | plate... |
| planina | bulgarian | mounta... |
| puig | catalonian | pe... |
| pulau | indonesian, malay | isla... |
| puncak | indonesian | pe... |
| puy | french | pe... |

## Q

| | | |
|---|---|---|
| qundao | chinese | archipela... |

## R

| | | |
|---|---|---|
| represa | portugese | dam, reserv... |
| retto | japanese | archipela... |
| rio | portugese, spanish | riv... |

## S

| | | |
|---|---|---|
| sabkhat | arabic | salt mar... |
| sadd | arabic | da... |
| sahra | arabic | dese... |
| salar | spanish | salt p... |
| san | japanese, korean | mounta... |
| sanmaek | korean | mountain ran... |
| sebkha | arabic | salt p... |
| sebkhet | arabic | salt mar... |
| sebkra | arabic | salt p... |
| see | german | se... |
| serra | portugese | mountain ran... |
| sha'ib | arabic | watercour... |
| shamo | chinese | dese... |
| shan | chinese | mountain, mountain ran... |
| shima | japanese | islan... |
| shoto | japanese | islan... |
| sierra | spanish | mountain ran... |
| sistema(s) | spanish | system... |

## T

| | | |
|---|---|---|
| ténéré | berber | des... |
| to | japanese | isla... |

## V

| | | |
|---|---|---|
| vesi | finnish | la... |
| vdkhr., vodokhranilishche | russian | reservo... |
| vírful | romanian | mounta... |
| volcan | spanish | volca... |

## W

| | | |
|---|---|---|
| wadi | arabic | watercour... |
| wald | german | fore... |

## Y

| | | |
|---|---|---|
| yam | hebrew | lak... |

# The Mini
# Satellite Atlas
## OF THE
# WORLD

## Using the Index

All the placenames and features appearing in this atlas are included in this index. The same feature name may appear on several different pages. In order to avoid duplication, the name will generally be referred to the largest scale map on which the feature appears.

Placename or feature name ———— **Antigua and Barbuda** Caribbean A 93 M5

Country or group of countries
within which the name appears

Symbols to indicate the type of
feature (see box below)

Page number ————

Grid reference ———— **K9**

---

### Explanation of symbols used

| | | | |
|---|---|---|---|
| ◉ | Physical region, feature | ■ | Capital City |
| ⬚ | Island or Island group, Rocky reef, Coral reef | ◉ | State capital |
| ▲ | Mountain, volcano, peak | Ⓐ | Country names |
| | Mountain range | | State or province name |
| ⬗ | Cape, point | ◭ | Lake or salt lake |
| ⟋ | River, canal | ◺ | Sea, ocean |
| ◉ | Place name | ◿ | Gulf, strait, bay |
| | | ✳ | Point/Place of interest |

**A**

Aachen *Germany* 25 B6
Abadan *Iran* 43 C1
Abéché *Chad* 48 D5
Aberdeen *United Kingdom* 14 M4
Abez *Russia* 21 N1
Abidjan *Côte d'Ivoire* 50 D5
Abu Dhabi (Abu Zabi)
   *United Arab Emirates* 43 E4
Abu Zabi (Abu Dhabi)
   *United Arab Emirates* 43 E4
Abuja *Nigeria* 51 F3
Acapulco *Mexico* 92 E5
Accra *Ghana* 50 D3
Açores (Azores) *Portugal* 46 (1)B2
Ad Dahna *Saudi Arabia* 40 E4
Ad Dakhla *Western Sahara* 46 B4
Ad Dammam *Saudi Arabia* 43 D3
Ad Dawhah (Doha) *Qatar* 43 D4
Adan (Aden) *Yemen* 40 E7
Adana *Turkey* 27 N4
Adapazarı *Turkey* 27 N4
Adelaide *Australia* 75 G6
Aden (Adan) *Yemen* 40 E7
Adis Abeba (Addis Ababa) *Ethiopia* 53 F2
Adriatic Sea *Europe* 38 D3
Aegean Sea *Europe* 36 G5
Afghanistan *Asia* 41 H3
Agadez *Niger* 47 G5
Agadir *Morocco* 46 D2
Ahmadabad *India* 62 B4
Ahvaz *Iran* 43 C1
Air (Azbine) *Niger* 47 G5
Ajaccio (Corsica) *France* 32 C7
Akita *Japan* 69 L4
Akmola *Kazakhstan* 59 N7
Aktyubinsk *Kazakhstan* 21 M4
Al Bahr al Mayyi (Dead Sea) *Jordan* 42 C5
Al Basrah (Basra) *Iraq* 43 B3
Al Furat (Euphrates) *Middle East* 40 C2
Al Haruj al Aswad *Libya* 48 C3
Al Hasa' *Saudi Arabia* 43 C3
Al Hijaz *Saudi Arabia* 40 C4
Al Jabal al Akhdar *Oman* 43 G4
Al Khufrah *Libya* 48 D4
Al Khufrah *Libya* 48 D4
Al Kuwayt (Kuwait) *Kuwait* 43 C2
Al Madinah (Medina) *Saudi Arabia* 40 C5
Al Manamah (Manama) *Bahrain* 43 D3
Al Mawsil (Mosul) *Iraq* 40 D2
Alabama *United States* 90 D2
Åland (Ahvenanmaa) *Finland* 19 L6
Åland Hav *Sweden* 19 L6
Alaska *United States* 88 (1)G2
Alaska Range *United States* 88 (1)G3
Albacete *Spain* 29 J5
Albania *Europe* 36 B4
Albany *United States* 87 F2
Alberta *Canada* 80 H5
Ålborg *Denmark* 19 E8
Albuquerque *United States* 89 E1
Alenuihaha Channel *United States* 89 (2)E4
Aleppo (Halab) *Syria* 40 C2
Ålesund *Norway* 19 D5
Aleutian Islands *United States* 88 (3)B1
Alexander Archipelago
   *United States* 88 (1)K4
Alexandria (El Iskandariyah) *Egypt* 49 E1
Alger (Algiers) *Algeria* 47 F1
Algeria *Africa* 47 E3
Algiers (Alger) *Algeria* 47 F1
Alicante *Spain* 29 K6
Alice Springs *Australia* 74 F4
Almaty *Kazakhstan* 58 P9
Almería *Spain* 29 H8
Alps *Europe* 27 M8
Amanab *Papua New Guinea* 71 F3
Amarillo *United States* 89 F1
Amazonas (Amazon) *Brazil* 96 E4
Ambon *Indonesia* 71 C3
American Highland *Antarctica* 100
American Samoa (U.S.) *Oceania* 73 K7
Amery Ice Shelf *Antarctica* 100 (2)M2

Amiens *France* 26 H4
Amirante Islands *Seychelles* 55 (2)B2
Amman *Jordan* 42 D4
Amsterdam *Netherlands* 17 J2
Amundsen Sea *Antarctica* 100 (2)GG4
Amur (Heilong Jiang) *China / Russia* 60 M6
An Nasiriyah *Iraq* 43 B1
Anchorage *United States* 88 (1)H3
Ancona *Italy* 31 J7
Andaman Islands (India) *Indian Ocean* 63 F6
Andaman Sea *South East Asia* 64 B4
Andorra *Europe* 23 G11
Andorra la Vella *Andorra* 27 G11
Andreanof Islands *United States* 88 (3)C1
Andros *Bahamas* 91 F5
Andros *Greece* 36 G7
Angarsk *Russia* 60 G6
Anglesey *United Kingdom* 15 J8
Angola *Southern Africa* 54 B2
Anguilla (U.K.) *Caribbean* 93 M5
Ankara *Turkey* 39 E4
Annaba *Algeria* 47 G1
Annapolis *United States* 87 E3
Annobón (Pagalu) *Equatorial Guinea* 51 F5
Anshan *China* 67 G2
Antalya *Turkey* 39 D4
Antananarivo *Madagascar* 55 H3
Anti-Atlas *Morocco* 46 D3
Antigua and Barbuda *Caribbean* 93 M5
Antipodes Islands *New Zealand* 77 (3)B1
Antofagasta *Chile* 98 G3
Antsiranana *Madagascar* 55 H2
Antwerpen *Belgium* 17 H3
Apeldoorn *Netherlands* 24 A4
Appalachian Mountains *United States* 87 D3
Appennino (Apennines) *Italy* 32 E4
Appennino Meridionale *Italy* 34 G8
Aqaba *Jordan* 42 C7
Ar Riyad (Riyadh) *Saudi Arabia* 40 E5
Arabian Sea *Middle East* 41 H6
Arad *Romania* 35 J3
Arafura Sea *Oceania* 72 D6
Araks *Middle East* 43 D1
Aral Sea (Aral'skoye More)
   *Kazakhstan / Uzbekistan* 59 K9
Aral'skoye More (Aral Sea)
   *Kazakhstan / Uzbekistan* 59 K9
Aras *Asia* 39 M4
Archangel *Russia* 20 J2
Archipel des Comores *Comoros* 55 G2
Archipelago of the Recherche
   *Australia* 74 D6
Arctic Ocean *Arctic* 100 (1)KK1
Ardennes *Belgium* 17 J4
Arequipa *Peru* 96 C7
Åreskutan *Sweden* 18 G5
Argentil *France* 26 F6
Argentina *South America* 98 H4
Arges *Romania* 35 N5
Argonne *France* 17 J5
Arizona *United States* 88 D2
Arkalyk *Kazakhstan* 21 P4
Arkansas *United States* 90 C2
Arkansas River *United States* 90 C2
Arlon *Belgium* 17 J4
Armenia *Asia* 39 M4
Arnhem *Netherlands* 17 J3
Arras *France* 16 F4
As Sahra' al Libiyah (Libyan Desert)
   *Libya* 48 D2
As Sahra' an Nubiyah (Nubian Desert)
   *Sudan* 49 F3
As Sahra' ash Sharqiyah (Eastern Desert)
   *Egypt* 49 F2
As Sudd *Sudan* 52 D2
Asahikawa *Japan* 69 M2
Ash Shariqah (Sharjah)
   *United Arab Emirates* 43 F4
Ashford *United Kingdom* 16 D3
Ashgabat (Ashkhabad) *Turkmenistan* 41 G3
Ashkhabad (Ashgabat) *Turkmenistan* 41 G3
Asir *Saudi Arabia* 40 D5
Asmara *Eritrea* 49 G4

Astove Group *Seychelles* 55 (2)A3
Astrachan *Russia* 21 K5
Asunción *Paraguay* 99 K4
Aswân *Egypt* 49 F3
Asyût *Egypt* 49 F2
Atâr *Mauritania* 46 C4
Athabasca Lake *Canada* 80 J5
Athína (Athínai) *Greece* 37 E7
Athínai (Athens) *Greece* 36 H7
Atlanta *United States* 91 E3
Atlantic Ocean *Europe* 12 B3
Atyrau *Kazakhstan* 21 L5
Auckland *New Zealand* 76 E3
Auckland Islands *New Zealand* 77 (2)B1
Augsburg *Germany* 25 F8
Augusta *United States* 87 G2
Austin *United States* 90 B3
Australia *Oceania* 74 F4
Australian Capital Territory *Australia* 75 J7
Austria *Europe* 31 K3
Awanui *New Zealand* 76 D2
Axios *Greece* 36 E4
Ayers Rock *Australia* 74 F5
'Ayoûn el Atroûs *Mauritania* 46 D5
Azbine (Air) *Niger* 47 G5
Azerbaijan *Asia* 39 M3
Azores (Açores) *Portugal* 46 (1)B2

**B**

Babuyan Islands *Philippines* 65 G3
Bacolod *Philippines* 65 G4
Badajoz *Spain* 28 D6
Badiet esh Sham (Syrian Desert) *Syria* 42 E3
Baffin Bay *North America* 81 T2
Baffin Island *Canada* 81 Q2
Bagdad (Baghdad) *Iraq* 40 D3
Baghdad (Bagdad) *Iraq* 40 D3
Bahamas *Atlantic Ocean* 91 F4
Bahía Blanca *Argentina* 98 J6
Bahía de Campeche *Mexico* 92 F4
Bahrain *Middle East* 43 D3
Baie de la Seine *France* 26 B4
Baile Átha Cliath (Dublin) *Ireland* 15 G8
Baja California *Mexico* 92 B3
Bakersfield *United States* 89 C1
Bakhtaran *Iran* 38 N6
Baki (Baku) *Azerbaijan* 39 P3
Baku (Baki) *Azerbaijan* 39 P3
Balıkesir *Turkey* 37 K5
Balabac *Philippines* 65 F5
Balearic Isles (Islas Baleares) *Spain* 29 N5
Balikpapan *Indonesia* 70 F3
Baltic Sea *Europe* 19 J9
Baltimore *United States* 87 E3
Bamako *Mali* 50 C2
Banaadir *Somalia* 53 G3
Banda Sea *Indonesia* 71 C4
Bandar Seri Begawan *Brunei* 70 E2
Bandar-e 'Abbas *Iran* 43 G3
Bandar-e Lengeh *Iran* 43 F3
Bandung *Indonesia* 70 D4
Bangalore *India* 63 C6
Bangkok (Krung Thep) *Thailand* 64 C4
Bangladesh *Southern Asia* 62 E4
Bangui *Central African Republic* 52 B3
Banjarmasin *Indonesia* 70 E3
Banjul *Gambia* 46 B6
Banks Island *Canada* 80 G2
Banks Peninsula *New Zealand* 77 D6
Baotou *China* 66 E2
Barbados *Caribbean* 93 N6
Barcelona *Spain* 29 N3
Barents Sea *Northern Europe* 58 D3
Bari *Italy* 33 L7
Barkly Tableland *Australia* 75 G3
Barnaul *Russia* 59 Q7
Barquisimeto *Venezuela* 96 D1
Barranquilla *Colombia* 96 C1
Basel *Switzerland* 30 C3
Basildon *United Kingdom* 16 D3
Basra (Al Basrah) *Iraq* 43 B1
Bass Strait *Australia* 75 H8

...stogne Belgium 17 J4
Batangas Philippines 65 G4
Bon Rouge United States 90 C3
y of Bengal India 63 E5
y of Biscay France / Spain 27 C9
y of Plenty New Zealand 76 F3
veux France 16 C3
berley Head United Kingdom 16 P11
aufort Sea North Pole 80 E2
aumont United States 90 C3
jijing China 66 F2
ira Mozambique 55 E3
irut (Beyrouth) Lebanon 42 C3
lsy Moldova 35 R2
limopan Belize 92 G5
o Horizonte Brazil 97 J7
loye More (White Sea) Russia 20 H1
n Nevis United Kingdom 14 H5
mo (Banghazi) Libya 48 C1
ni-Abbès Algeria 47 J5
am West Africa 51 E2
ranchs City Nigeria 51 F3
lgorad (Belgrade) Yugoslavia 34 H5
erenki Russia 98 N4
rgen Norway 19 C6
ring Sea Pacific Ocean 88 (1)C3
ringov Proliv / Bering Strait
   Russia / United States 88 (1)D2
rlevåg Norway 18 Q1
rlin Germany 24 J4
rn Switzerland 30 C4
rnay France 16 D5
opal India 62 C4
utan Southern Asia 62 F3
alystok Poland 22 N4
elefeld Germany 24 D4
alsko-Biała Poland 23 J8
ao Bosnia-Herzegovina 34 C5
agan Spain 28 H1
dovo Bosnia-Herzegovina 34 E6
ao Central African Republic 52 C1
rmingham United Kingdom 15 M9
rmingham United States 91 D4
shkek Kyrgyzstan 59 N9
smarck United States 85 F1
smarck Sea Papua New Guinea 72 E6
ssau Guinea-Bissau 50 A2
tola Macedonia 35 J6
rnevatn Norway 18 Q2
ck Rock Desert United States 84 C2
ck Sea Europe 39 Q2
entyre Malaysia 55 E3
da Algeria 29 N8
emfontein South Africa 54 D5
ue Nile Sudan 49 B7
   Sierra Leone 50 B3
Hai China 67 F3
bo Dioulasso Burkina Faso 50 D2
boruysk Belarus 20 F4
chum Germany 24 C5
hole Chile 47 J5
densee Germany / Switzerland 25 E9
de Norway 18 H3
gotá Colombia 96 C3
hol Sea Philippines 65 G5
se United States 84 C2
lgatanga Ghana 50 D2
logna Italy 32 F4
naparte Archipelago Australia 74 D3
nn Germany 25 C6
rdeaux France 27 E9
rneo South East Asia 70 E2
rnholm Denmark 22 D2

Bosnia-Herzegovina Europe 34 E5
Bosporus (Karadeniz Bogazi) Turkey 39 C3
Bossangoa Central African Republic 51 H3
Boston United States 87 F2
Botswana Southern Africa 54 C4
Bouaké Côte D'Ivoire 50 D3
Boulogne France 16 C3
Brac Croatia 34 D6
Brahmaputra Southern Asia 62 E3
Braila Romania 35 Q4
Brasília Brazil 97 H7
Brasov Romania 35 N4
Bratislava Slovakia 23 G9
Bratsk Russia 60 D2
Braunschweig Germany 24 F4
Brazil South America 94 F4
Brazilian Highlands (Planalto do Brasil)
   Brazil 97 J7
Brazzaville Congo 51 G5
Brecon Beacons United Kingdom 15 K10
Bremen Germany 24 D3
Bremerhaven Germany 24 D3
Brescia Italy 32 E4
Brest Belarus 20 E4
Brest France 26 A5
Bridgetown Barbados 93 N6
Brighton United Kingdom 16 N11
Brisbane Australia 75 K5
Bristol United Kingdom 15 L10
Bristol Channel United Kingdom 15 J10
British Columbia Canada 80 F5
Brno Czech Republic 23 F8
Brugge Belgium 16 G3
Brunei Asia 70 F2
Brussels (Brüssel / Bruxelles) Belgium 17 H4
Bruxelles / Brüssel (Brussels) Belgium 17 H4
Bryansk Russia 20 G4
Bucharest (Bucuresti) Romania 35 P5
Bucuresti (Bucharest) Romania 35 P5
Budapest Hungary 34 G2
Buenos Aires Argentina 99 K5
Buffalo United States 87 E2
Bujumbura Burundi 52 D4
Bukavu Democratic Republic of Congo 52 D4
Bulawayo Zimbabwe 54 D4
Bulgan Mongolia 66 C2
Bulgaria Europe 35 L7
Bumba Democratic Republic of Congo 52 C3
Bunbury Australia 74 C6
Bür Sa'īd (Port Said) Egypt 49 H1
Bur Sudan (Port Sudan) Sudan 49 G4
Burgas Bulgaria 35 Q7
Burgos Spain 28 G2
Burkina Faso West Africa 50 D2
Bursa Turkey 39 C3
Burundi Central Africa 52 D4
Bushehr Iran 43 D2
Büyük Agri Dagi (Mount Ararat) Turkey 39 L4
Bydgoszcz Poland 22 F4
Bytom Poland 23 H7

C
Cabanatuan Philippines 65 G3
Cabinda Angola 51 G6
Cabo de São Roque Brazil 98 H10
Cabo de São Vicente Portugal 28 A8
Cabo Trafalgar Spain 28 D8
Cádiz Spain 28 D8
Caen France 16 C4
Cagayan de Oro Philippines 65 G5
Cagliari (Sardinia) Italy 33 D9
Cairo (El Qâhira) Egypt 49 F2
Calais France 26 G3
Calamian Group Philippines 65 F4
Calcutta India 62 E4
Cali Colombia 96 B3
California United States 88 C1
Cambodia South East Asia 64 C4
Cambrian Mountains United Kingdom 15 J10
Cambridge United Kingdom 15 P9
Cameroon West Africa 51 G4

Campbell Island New Zealand 77 (2)C2
Campinas Brazil 97 H8
Campo Grande Brazil 97 G8
Campos Brazil 97 J8
Canada North America 80 K4
Canal de Panama (Panama Canal)
   Panama 93 J7
Canale di Corsica Italy 32 B6
Canary Islands (Islas Canarias) (Sp.)
   Atlantic Ocean 46 B3
Canberra Australia 75 J7
Canterbury Bight New Zealand 77 D7
Canterbury Plains New Zealand 77 C6
Canton (Guangzhou) China 66 E6
Cap Bengut Algeria 47 F1
Cap Bon Italy 33 F11
Cap Bon Tunisia 47 H1
Cap d'Antifer France 16 D5
Cap Gris-Nez France 16 E4
Cape Agulhas South Africa 54 C6
Cape Canaveral United States 91 E4
Cape Clear Ireland 15 D11
Cape Cod United States 87 G2
Cape Comorin India 63 C7
Cape Farewell New Zealand 77 C5
Cape Horn (Cabo de Hornos) Chile 98 H10
Cape Inscription Australia 74 B5
Cape Leeuwin Australia 74 B6
Cape Maria Van Diemen
   New Zealand 76 B2
Cape of Good Hope South Africa 54 B6
Cape Palliser New Zealand 77 E5
Cape Sable United States 91 E5
Cape Verde Atlantic Ocean 50 (1)B2
Cape Wessel Australia 75 G2
Cape Wrath United Kingdom 14 H3
Cape York Australia 75 H2
Capetown South Africa 54 B6
Capricorn Group Australia 75 K4
Caracas Venezuela 96 D1
Cardiff United Kingdom 15 K10
Cardigan Bay United Kingdom 15 J9
Caribbean Sea Central America 93 J5
Carnsore Point Ireland 15 G9
Caroline Islands (Micronesia) Oceania 72 E5
Carpathian Mountains
   Ukraine / Romania 35 M1
Carpathians (Západné Karpaty)
   Slovakia 23 H9
Carpati Meridionali Romania 35 K4
Carpati Occidentali Romania 23 M11
Carrantuohill Ireland 15 D10
Carson City United States 84 C3
Cartagena Colombia 96 B1
Cartagena Spain 29 K7
Casablanca (Dar-el-Beida) Morocco 46 D2
Cascade Range United States 84 B2
Caspian Sea Europe 39 N2
Castellón de la Plana Spain 29 K4
Catània Sicily 33 K11
Caucasus Asia 39 J2
Cauvery India 63 C6
Cavalli Islands New Zealand 76 D2
Cayenne French Guiana 97 G3
Cebu Philippines 65 G4
Cedar Rapids United States 86 B3
Celebes Sea Indonesia 71 H2
Celebes (Sulawesi) Indonesia 71 A3
Celtic Sea United Kingdom 15 E10
Central African Republic Central Africa 52 D4
Central Siberian Plain (Srednesibirskoye
   Ploskogoryn) Russia 60 F4
Ceram (Seram) Indonesia 71 C3
Cerro Aconcagua Argentina 98 G8
Ceuta Spain 28 E9
Ch'ongjin North Korea 68 E3
Chad West Africa 48 C4
Challenger Deep Oceania 72 E4
Chang Jiang China 66 F4
Changbai Shan East Asia 68 D3
Changchun China 67 H2
Changsha China 66 E5
Channel Islands United Kingdom 15 K12
Channel Islands United States 88 C2

Chao Phraya *South East Asia* ▣ 64 C3
Chardzhou *Turkmenistan* ▣ 59 L10
Charleroi *Belgium* ▣ 17 H4
Charleston *United States* ▣ 91 E2
Charlotte *United States* ▣ 91 D3
Charlottetown *Canada* ▣ 81 U7
Chatham Islands *New Zealand* ▣ 77 (1)B2
Chattanooga *United States* ▣ 91 D2
Cheju-Do (Quelpart I.) *South Korea* ▣ 68 D7
Chelyabinsk *Russia* ▣ 21 N3
Chemnitz *Germany* ▣ 25 J6
Chengdu *China* ▣ 66 C4
Chengdu Qiling *China* ▣ 66 C4
Chennai / Madras *India* ▣ 63 D6
Cherbourg *France* ▣ 16 D4
Cherepovets *Russia* ▣ 20 H3
Chernigov *Ukraine* ▣ 20 G4
Chernovtsy *Ukraine* ▣ 20 F5
Cheyenne *United States* ▣ 85 F2
Chicago *United States* ▣ 90 C2
Chiclayo *Peru* ▣ 96 B5
Chihuahua *Mexico* ▣ 89 E3
Chile *South America* ▣ 98 H4
Chiltern Hills *United Kingdom* ▣ 15 M10
Chimkent *Kazakhstan* ▣ 59 M9
China *East Asia* ▣ 66 B4
Chingola *Zambia* ▣ 54 D2
Chisinau *Moldova* ▣ 20 F5
Chita *Russia* ▣ 60 J6
Chittagong *Bangladesh* ▣ 62 F4
Chongqing *China* ▣ 66 D5
Chonju *South Korea* ▣ 68 D6
Christchurch *New Zealand* ▣ 77 D6
Christmas Island *Australia* ▣ 70 D5
Cincinnati *United States* ▣ 86 D3
Ciltaltépetl *Mexico* ▣ 92 E5
Ciudad de Mexico (Mexico City)

          *Mexico* ▣ 92 D5
Ciudad Guayana *Venezuela* ▣ 94 C9
Ciudad Juárez *Mexico* ▣ 92 C2
Clermont-Ferrand *France* ▣ 27 J8
Cleveland *United States* ▣ 86 D2
Cluj Napoca *Romania* ▣ 35 L3
Coast Mountains *Canada* ▣ 80 F6
Coast Range *United States* ▣ 84 B2
Coimbatore *India* ▣ 63 C6
Colchester *United Kingdom* ▣ 16 D3
Collines de Normandie *France* ▣ 16 C6
Collines du Perche *France* ▣ 16 D6
Collingham *United Kingdom* ▣ 15 N8
Cologne (Köln) *Germany* ▣ 25 B6
Colombia *South America* ▣ 96 C3
Colombo *Sri Lanka* ▣ 63 C7
Colorado *United States* ▣ 85 E3
Colorado Plateau *United States* ▣ 84 D3
Colorado River *United States* ▣ 85 F3
Columbia *United States* ▣ 91 E3
Columbia Mountains *Canada* ▣ 80 G6
Columbia River *United States* ▣ 84 B1
Columbus *United States* ▣ 86 D3
Comoros *Indian Ocean* ▣ 55 G2
Comrat *Moldova* ▣ 35 P3
Conakry *Guinea* ▣ 50 B3
Concepción *Chile* ▣ 98 G6
Concord *United States* ▣ 87 F2
Congo *West Africa* ▣ 51 H4
Connecticut *United States* ▣ 87 F2
Constanta *Romania* ▣ 35 R5
Cook Islands *N. Z.) Oceania* ▣ 73 K7
Cook Strait *New Zealand* ▣ 76 E5
Copenhagen (Kebnhavn) *Denmark* ▣ 19 F9
Coral Sea *Australia* ▣ 75 K2
Coral Sea Islands Territory *Micronesia* ▣ 72 E7
Cordillera Cantábrica *Spain* ▣ 28 D2
Cordillera Los Andes *South America* ▣ 96 B5
Cordillera Occidental *Colombia* ▣ 96 B3
Córdoba *Argentina* ▣ 98 J5
Córdoba *Spain* ▣ 28 F7
Corfu (Kérkira) *Greece* ▣ 36 B5
Cork *Ireland* ▣ 15 E10
Corno Grande *Italy* ▣ 32 H4
Corpus Christi *United States* ▣ 90 B4
Corrientes *Argentina* ▣ 99 K4

Corse (Corsica) (Fr.) *Mediterranean* ▣ 32 C6
Corsica (Corse) (Fr.) *Mediterranean* ▣ 32 C6
Cosenza *Italy* ▣ 33 L9
Cosmoledo Group *Seychelles* ▣ 55 (2)A2
Costa Rica *Central America* ▣ 93 G6
Côte d'Ivoire *West Africa* ▣ 50 C4
Coventry *United Kingdom* ▣ 16 B2
Craiova *Romania* ▣ 35 L5
Crete (Kriti) *Greece* ▣ 36 G9
Cristobal Colón *Colombia* ▣ 96 C1
Croatia *Europe* ▣ 34 D4
Cuba *Caribbean* ▣ 93 H4
Cúcuta *Colombia* ▣ 96 C2
Cudskoje ozero / Peipsi järv

          *Estonia / Russia* ▣ 19 P7
Culiacán Rosales *Mexico* ▣ 92 C4
Curitiba *Brazil* ▣ 99 M4
Cuzco *Peru* ▣ 96 C6
Cyclades (Kyklades) *Greece* ▣ 36 G7
Cyprus *Europe* ▣ 37 Q9
Czech Republic *Europe* ▣ 23 D8
Czestochówa *Poland* ▣ 23 J7

## D

Da Nang *Vietnam* ▣ 64 D3
Dakar *Senegal* ▣ 46 A6
Dalian *China* ▣ 67 G3
Dallas *United States* ▣ 90 B3
Damascus (Dimashq) *Syria* ▣ 42 D3
Dandong *China* ▣ 67 G2
Danube (Donau) *Europe* ▣ 30 G2
Danube (Donau) *Europe* ▣ 23 G10
Danzig (Gdansk) *Poland* ▣ 22 H3
Dar es Salaam *Tanzania* ▣ 53 F5
Dar Rounga *Central Africa* ▣ 52 C2
Dar-el-Beida (Casablanca) *Morocco* ▣ 46 D2
Dardanelles *Turkey* ▣ 37 J4
Darling River *Australia* ▣ 75 H6
Darmstadt *Germany* ▣ 17 J5
Dartmoor *United Kingdom* ▣ 15 K11
Darwin *Australia* ▣ 74 F2
Daryacheh-ye Orumiyeh *Iran* ▣ 39 L5
Dasht-e-Lut *Iran* ▣ 43 H5
Daugavpils *Latvia* ▣ 19 P9
Davao *Philippines* ▣ 65 H5
Davenport *United States* ▣ 86 B2
Davis Sea *Antarctica* ▣ 100 (2)Q3
Dawad Sea (Al Bahr al Mayyi) *Jordan* ▣ 42 C5
Dead Sea (Yam Ha Melah) *Israel* ▣ 42 C5
Death Valley *United States* ▣ 84 C3
Debrecen *Hungary* ▣ 34 J2
Deccan *India* ▣ 63 C5
Delaware *United States* ▣ 87 F3
Delhi *India* ▣ 62 C3
Democratic Republic of Congo

          *Central Africa* ▣ 52 C4
Den Haag ('s-Gravenhage) (The Hague)

          *Netherlands* ▣ 17 H2
Den Helder *Netherlands* ▣ 17 H2
Denizli *Turkey* ▣ 37 M5
Denmark *Europe* ▣ 19 D9
Denver *United States* ▣ 85 F3
Derby *United Kingdom* ▣ 16 B2
Des Moines *United States* ▣ 86 B2
Dessau *Germany* ▣ 24 H5
Detroit *United States* ▣ 86 D2
Deutsche Bucht *North Sea* ▣ 24 E2
Deva *Romania* ▣ 35 K3
Deyyer *Iran* ▣ 43 D3
Dhaka *Bangladesh* ▣ 62 F4
Dieppe *France* ▣ 16 D4
Dijlah (Tigris) *Middle East* ▣ 40 E3
Dijon *France* ▣ 26 L6
Dimashq (Damascus) *Syria* ▣ 42 D3
Dinara *Bosnia-Herzegovina / Croatia* ▣ 34 D5
District of Columbia (D.C.)

          *United States* ▣ 87 E3
Diyarbakır *Turkey* ▣ 39 J5
Djanet *Algeria* ▣ 47 H4
Djibouti *Djibouti* ▣ 49 H5
Djibouti *North East Africa* ▣ 49 H5

Dnepropetrovsk *Ukraine* ▣ 20 H5
Dobrich *Bulgaria* ▣ 35 Q6
Dodecanes (Dodekánissa) *Greece* ▣ 36 J7
Dodekánissa (Dodecanes) *Greece* ▣ 36 J7
Dodoma *Tanzania* ▣ 53 F5
Dogger Bank *United Kingdom* ▣ 15 Q7
Doha (Ad Dawhah) *Qatar* ▣ 43 D4
Dominica *Caribbean* ▣ 93 M5
Dominican Republic *Caribbean* ▣ 93 K5
Donau (Danube) *Europe* ▣ 30 G2
Donegal Bay *Ireland* ▣ 15 E7
Donegal Mountains *Ireland* ▣ 15 E7
Donetsk *Ukraine* ▣ 20 H5
Dong Hai / Higashi-Shina-Kai (East China Sea)

          *South East Asia* ▣ 67 H5
Dongnan Qiuling *China* ▣ 66 E6
Dorotea *Sweden* ▣ 18 J4
Dortmund *Germany* ▣ 24 C5
Dover *United Kingdom* ▣ 15 Q10
Dover *United States* ▣ 87 E3
Drake Passage *South America* ▣ 98 G10
Drakensberg *South Africa / Lesotho* ▣ 54 D6
Drava *Europe* ▣ 32 L2
Dresden *Germany* ▣ 25 J5
Drift Prairie *United States* ▣ 85 G1
Dubai (Dubayy) *United Arab Emirates* ▣ 43 F4
Dubayy (Dubai) *United Arab Emirates* ▣ 43 F4
Dublin (Baile Atha Cliath) *Ireland* ▣ 15 H8
Dugi Otok *Croatia* ▣ 34 C5
Duisburg *Germany* ▣ 24 B5
Duluth *United States* ▣ 86 B1
Dumont d'Urville Sea *Antarctica* ▣ 100 (2)U3
Duna *Hungary* ▣ 34 F3
Dunaj (Danube) *Europe* ▣ 23 G10
Dunedin *New Zealand* ▣ 77 C7
Dunaj (Danube) *Europe* ▣ 23 G10
Dunga *Democratic Republic of Congo* ▣ 52 D1
Dunkerque *France* ▣ 16 F3
Dunnet Head *United Kingdom* ▣ 14 K3
Durban *South Africa* ▣ 54 E5
Durrës *Albania* ▣ 36 B3
Dushanbe *Tajikistan* ▣ 41 J2
Düsseldorf *Germany* ▣ 25 B5
Dzhezkazgan *Kazakhstan* ▣ 59 M8

## E

East Cape *New Zealand* ▣ 76 G3
East China Sea (Dong Hai / Higashi-Shina-Kai)

          *South East Asia* ▣ 67 H5
East London *South Africa* ▣ 54 D6
East Siberian Sea (Vostocno-Sibirskoye More)

          *Russia* ▣ 61 S3
Easter Island (Chile) *Pacific Ocean* ▣ 73 Q8
Eastern Desert (As Sahra ash Sharqiyah)

          *Egypt* ▣ 49
Eastern Ghats *India* ▣ 63 D5
Eben *Spain* ▣ 29 N3
Ech Cheliff *Algeria* ▣ 29 M8
Ecuador *South America* ▣ 96 B4
Edinburgh *United Kingdom* ▣ 14 K6
Edmonton *Canada* ▣ 80 J6
Egypt *North Africa* ▣ 48 E3
Eifel *Germany* ▣ 25 B6
Eight Degree Channel *Arabian Sea* ▣ 63 B7
Eindhoven *Netherlands* ▣ 17 J3
El Giza (Giza) *Egypt* ▣ 49 F2
El Goléa *Algeria* ▣ 47 F2
El Iskandariyah (Alexandria) *Egypt* ▣ 49 E1
El Khartum (Khartoum) *Sudan* ▣ 49 F4
El Qâhira (Cairo) *Egypt* ▣ 49 E2
El Salvador *Central America* ▣ 92 F6
Elba *Italy* ▣ 32 E6
Elbasan *Albania* ▣ 36 C3
Elbe (Labe)

          *Germany / Czech Republic* ▣ 25 H3
Elbląg *Poland* ▣ 22 J3
Elburz *Iran* ▣ 39 N5
Elche *Spain* ▣ 29 K6
Ellice Islands (Tuvalu) *Oceania* ▣ 72 H6
Emi Koussi *Chad* ▣ 48 C4
Ems *Germany* ▣ 24 C4
Enontekiö *Finland* ▣ 18 M2
Engels *Russia* ▣ 20 K4
England *United Kingdom* ▣ 15 L9

nglish Channel / La Manche
    *United Kingdom / France* ▣ 15 L11
nedi *Chad* ▣ 48 D4
nnedi *Chad* 🇹 17 G5
quatorial Guinea *West Africa* ▣ 51 F4
biyas Dağı *Turkey* ◉ 39 F4
ntrea *Africa* ▣ 49 G4
rzurum *Turkey* ◉ 39 J4
  Semara *Western Sahara* 🇪 46 C3
chberg *Denmark* 🇩 19 F4
tona *Europe* ▣ 19 N7
kildtorp *Sweden* 🇸 19 J7
kilstuna *Sweden* 🗻 19 J7
kisehir *Turkey* ◉ 39 D4
bpo / Esbo *Finland* 🇫 19 N6
ben *Germany* ◉ 25 C5
tonia *Europe* ▣ 19 N7
tuario do Rio Amazonas *Brazil* 🇧 94 G3
nioua *Central Africa* 🇨 53 F2
la *Sicily* 🇮 33 J11
kildberg *United States* 🇺 84 B2
pratres (Al Furat) *Middle East* 🇲 40 C2
ansville *United States* 🇺 86 C3
reux *France* 🇫 16 E5
ber *United Kingdom* 🇬 15 K11
moor *United Kingdom* 🇬 16 K10

F
aeroes *Denmark* ▣ 12 D1
isalabad *Pakistan* ◉ 41 K3
kland *Indonesia* 🇮 71 D3
klkland Islands *South Atlantic Ocean* 🇫 99 K9
tan *Sweden* 🇸 19 H6
rrgo *United States* 🇺 85 G2
irquhar Group *Seychelles* 🇸 55 (2)B2
uzabad *Iran* 🇮 43 E2
thern Ranges *Australia* 🗻 75 G6
lt *United States* 🇺 86 C2
rence (Firenze) *Italy* 🗻 32 F5
bres Sea *Indonesia* 🇮 71 B4
rida *United States* 🇺 91 E4
rida Keys *United States* 🇺 91 E5
ggia *Italy* 🗻 33 K7
rli *Italy* 🗻 31 H6
rt Wayne *United States* 🇺 86 C2
rtaleza *Brazil* 🇧 94 H1
raleza *Brazil* 🇧 90 B3
aleza Strait *New Zealand* 🇳 77 A8
ance *Europe* ▣ 26 D6
ancistown *Botswana* 🗻 54 D4
nkfurt *Main* *Germany* 🇩 86 D3
nkfurt am Main *Germany* 🇩 25 F6
anz Josefland *Russia* 🇷 58 J1
dericton *Canada* 🇨 81 T7
etown *Sierra Leone* 🇸 50 B3
iburg im Breisgau *Germany* 🇩 25 C8
emantle *Australia* 🇦 74 C4
ench Guiana *South America* 🇫 97 G3
ench Polynesia (Fr.) *Oceania* 🇫 73 M7
ench Polynesia (Fr.) *Oceania* 🇫 84 C3
ji-San *Japan* 🇯 69 K6
kuoka *Japan* 🇯 68 F7
nabashi *Japan* 🇯 69 L6
meaux *Group Australia* 🗻 75 J8
shun *China* 🇨 67 G2
zhou *China* 🇨 67 G2
zhou *China* 🇨 67 F5

G
bes *Tunisia* 🇹 47 G2
abon *West Africa* ▣ 51 G5
aborone *Botswana* 🗻 54 D4
alapagos Islands (Islas Galápagos)
    *Ecuador* 🇪 96 (1)A1

Galati *Romania* ◉ 35 Q4
Gällivare *Sweden* 🇸 18 J3
Galway *Ireland* ◉ 15 E8
Galway Bay *Ireland* 🇮 15 D8
Gambia *West Africa* ▣ 50 A2
Ganga (Ganges) *Southern Asia* 🇮 62 D3
Ganges (Ganga) *Southern Asia* 🇮 62 D3
Garonne *France* 🇫 27 E9
Gawler Ranges *Australia* 🗻 75 G6
Gaza (Ghazzah) *Israel* 🇮 42 B5
Gaziantep *Turkey* ◉ 39 G5
Gdansk (Danzig) *Poland* ◉ 22 H3
Gdynia *Poland* ◉ 19 K9
Geelong *Australia* 🗻 75 H7
Gelsenkirchen *Germany* 🇩 24 C5
General Santos *Philippines* ◉ 65 H5
Geneva (Genève) *Switzerland* ◉ 30 A4
Geneva (Genève) *Switzerland* ◉ 30 A4
Genoa (Genova) *Italy* ◉ 32 C4
Genova (Genoa) *Italy* ◉ 32 C4
Gent *Belgium* ◉ 17 G3
Georgetown *Guyana* ◉ 97 F2
Georgia *Asia* ▣ 39 K3
Georgia *United States* ▣ 91 E3
Geraldton *Australia* 🇦 74 B5
Germany *Europe* ▣ 24 D4
Ghana *West Africa* ▣ 50 D3
Ghazzah (Gaza) *Israel* 🇮 42 B5
Gibraltar *United Kingdom* 🇬 28 E8
Gibson Desert *Australia* 🇦 74 D4
Gijón *Spain* ◉ 28 E1
Gilbert Islands (Kiribati) *Oceania* 🇴 72 H5
Gironde *France* 🗻 27 E8
Gisborne *New Zealand* ◉ 76 G4
Giza (El Giza) *Egypt* ◉ 49 E1
Glasgow *United Kingdom* ◉ 14 J6
Glazov *Russia* ◉ 21 L1
Glitterind *Norway* 🗻 19 E6
Gliwice *Poland* ◉ 23 H7
Gobi Desert *China / Mongolia* 🇨 66 D2
Godavari *India* 🇮 62 C5
Godthåb *Greenland* ◉ 81 W4
Golden Brazil *Brazil* ◉ 97 H7
Golden Gate *United States* 🇺 84 B3
Golfe de Alicante *Spain* 🇪 29 L6
Golfe de Almeria *Spain* 🇪 29 J8
Golfo de Cádiz *Spain / Portugal* 🇪 28 C8
Golfo de California *Mexico* 🇲 92 B3
Golfo de Mazarrón *Spain* 🇪 29 J7
Golfo de Rosas *Spain* 🇪 29 P2
Golfo de Valencia *Spain* 🇪 29 M5
Golfo de Génova *Italy* 🇮 32 C5
Golfo di Oristano *Italy* 🇮 33 B8
Golfo di Taranto *Italy* 🇮 33 L8
Golfo di Trieste *Italy* 🇮 32 H3
Golfo di Venezia *Italy* 🇮 32 H3
Gomel *Belarus* ◉ 20 G4
Gongga Shan *China* 🇨 66 C5
Gora Narodnaya *Russia* 🇷 21 N1
Gorki *Russia* ◉ 21 P1
Göteborg *Sweden* ◉ 19 F8
Governador Valadares *Brazil* ◉ 97 F7
Grampian Mountains *United Kingdom* 🇬 14 J5
Gran Chaco *Argentina / Paraguay* 🇦 98 J3
Granada *Spain* ◉ 28 G7
Grand Bahama *Bahamas* ◉ 91 F4
Grand Canyon *United States* 🇺 88 D1
Grand Erg de Bilma *Niger* 🇳 48 B4
Grand Erg Occidental *Algeria* 🇩 47 E3
Grand Erg Oriental *Algeria* 🇩 47 F3
Graz *Austria* ◉ 31 L3
Great Australian Bight *Australia* 🇦 74 E6
Great Barrier Island *New Zealand* 🇳 76 F3
Great Barrier Reef *Australia* 🗻 75 J3
Great Bear Lake *Canada* 🇨 80 D3
Great Dividing Range *Australia* 🗻 75 H3
Great Plains *United States* 🗻 85 F1
Great Prairies *United States* 🗻 89 F1
Great Salt Lake *United States* 🇺 84 D2
Great Salt Lake Desert *United States* 🗻 84 D6
Great Sandy Desert *Australia* 🇦 74 D4

Great Sandy Desert *United States* 🗻 84 B2
Great Slave Lake *Canada* 🇨 80 J4
Great Victoria Desert *Australia* 🇦 74 D5
Greater Antilles *Caribbean* 🇨 93 J4
Greater Sunda Islands *Indonesia* 🇮 70 E3
Greece *Europe* ▣ 36 D5
Greenland (Denmark)
    *North Atlantic Ocean* 🇩 81 X3
Greenland Sea *Iceland* 🇮 18 B1
Greensboro *United States* 🇺 91 F2
Grenada *Caribbean* ▣ 93 M6
Grenoble *France* ◉ 27 L8
Grey Range *Australia* 🗻 75 H5
Grimsstaðir *Iceland* 🇮 18 E2
Grodno *Belarus* ◉ 19 M10
Groningen *Netherlands* ◉ 17 K1
Groote Eylandt *Australia* 🇦 75 G2
Großglockner *Austria* 🗻 31 H3
Grozny (Groznyy) *Russia* ◉ 39 L2
Groznyy (Grosny) *Russia* ◉ 39 L2
Guadalajara *Mexico* ◉ 92 D4
Guadeloupe (Fr.) *Caribbean* 🇩 93 M5
Guam (U.S.) *Oceania* 🇴 72 E4
Guangzhou (Canton) *China* ◉ 66 E6
Guatemala *Central America* ▣ 92 F5
Guatemala City *Guatemala* ◉ 92 F6
Guayaquil *Ecuador* ◉ 96 A4
Guiana Highlands *South America* 🗻 96 E3
Guinea *West Africa* ▣ 50 B2
Guinea-Bissau *West Africa* ▣ 50 A2
Guiyang *China* ◉ 66 D5
Gulf of Aden *Middle East* 🇲 49 J5
Gulf of Alaska *North Pacific Ocean* 🇵 80 D5
Gulf of Aqaba *Saudi Arabia / Egypt* 🇸 42 B7
Gulf of Bothnia *Sweden / Finland* 🇸 18 K6
Gulf of Carpentaria *Australia* 🇦 75 G2
Gulf of Finland
    *Finland / Estonia / Russia* 🇫 19 N7
Gulf of Gdansk *Poland* 🇵 22 J3
Gulf of Guinea *Atlantic Ocean* 🇦 51 E4
Gulf of Kachchh *India* 🇮 62 A4
Gulf of Maine *United States* 🇺 81 T8
Gulf of Mexico *Central America* 🇨 92 F3
Gulf of Oman *Middle East* 🇲 41 G4
Gulf of Riga *Latvia* 🇱 19 M8
Gulf of St. Lawrence *Canada* 🇨 81 U7
Gulf of Thailand *South East Asia* 🇸 64 C4
Gulf of Tongking *South East Asia* 🇸 64 D2
Guyana *South America* ▣ 97 F3
Gvandzha *Azerbaijan* ◉ 39 M3
Győr *Hungary* ◉ 34 E2
Gyula *Hungary* ◉ 34 J3

H
Ha Nội (Hanoi) *Vietnam* ◉ 64 D2
Haarlem *Netherlands* ◉ 17 H2
Habana (Havana) *Cuba* ◉ 93 H4
Hagen *Germany* ◉ 25 C5
Haifa (Hefa) *Israel* ◉ 42 B4
Hainan *China* ▣ 66 D8
Haiphong *Vietnam* ◉ 64 D2
Haiti *Caribbean* ▣ 93 K5
Hakodate *Japan* ◉ 69 L3
Halab (Aleppo) *Syria* ◉ 40 C2
Halifax *Canada* ◉ 81 U8
Halle *Germany* ◉ 25 H5
Hamah *Syria* ◉ 38 G6
Hamamatsu *Japan* ◉ 69 J6
Hamburg *Germany* ◉ 24 F3
Hamersley Range *Australia* 🇦 74 C4
Hamhung *North Korea* ◉ 68 D4
Hami *China* ◉ 59 S9
Hamilton *Canada* ◉ 87 E2
Hamilton *New Zealand* ◉ 76 F3
Hammerfest *Norway* ◉ 18 M1
Handan *China* ◉ 66 E3
Hangzhou *China* ◉ 67 G4
Hannover *Germany* ◉ 24 E4
Hanoi (Ha Nội) *Vietnam* ◉ 64 D2
Harare *Zimbabwe* ◉ 55 S3
Harbin *China* ◉ 67 H1
Hargeysa *Somalia* ◉ 49 H6
Harrisburg *United States* ◉ 87 E2
Harstad *Norway* ◉ 18 J2

Hartford *United States* ● 87 F2
Harwich *United Kingdom* ● 16 E3
Harz *Germany* ▲ 17 F5
Haut Atlas *Morocco* ▲ 46 D2
Havana (Habana) *Cuba* ■ 93 H4
Hawaii *United States* ● 89 (2)E1
Hawaii *United States* ● 89 (2)G4
Hawaiian Islands *United States* 73 L3
Hefa (Haifa) *Israel* ● 42 B4
Hefei *China* ● 66 F4
Heilong Jiang (Amur) *China / Russia* ➳ 60 M6
Helena *United States* ■ 84 D1
Helsingborg *Sweden* ● 19 G8
Helsingfors (Helsinki) *Finland* ■ 19 N6
Helsinki (Helsingfors) *Finland* ■ 19 N6
Herat *Afghanistan* ● 41 H3
Hilo *United States* ● 89 (2)F4
Hims (Homs) *Syria* ● 42 C3
Hiroshima *Japan* ● 68 F6
Ho Chi Minh (Saigon) *Vietnam* ● 64 D4
Hobart *Australia* ■ 75 J8
Höfn *Iceland* ● 18 F2
Hohhot *China* ● 66 E2
Hok-Ku (Sea of Ochotsk) *East Asia* 69 M1
Hokkaido *Japan* ● 69 N2
Homs (Hims) *Syria* ● 42 C3
Honduras *Central America* ▲ 93 G6
Hong Kong *China* ● 66 E6
Honolulu *United States* ■ 89 (2)D2
Honshu *Japan* ● 69 L5
Hoogeveen *Netherlands* ● 17 K2
Houston *United States* ● 90 B4
Huainan *China* ● 66 F4
Huang Hai / Hwang-Hae (Yellow Sea)
   *South East Asia* 67 G3
Huang He *China* ➳ 66 F3
Huascaran *Peru* ▲ 96 B5
Hudson Bay *Canada* 81 P5
Hudson Strait *Canada* 81 S4
Huelva *Spain* ● 28 D7
Hungary *Europe* ▲ 23 H10
Huntsville *United States* ● 90 D3
Húsavík *Iceland* ● 18 E1
Hvar *Croatia* ● 34 D6
Hyderabad *India* ● 63 C5
Hyderabad *Pakistan* ● 41 J4

**I**
I-n-Guezzam *Algeria* ● 47 G5
Iasi *Romania* ● 35 Q2
Ibadan *Nigeria* ● 51 E3
Ibiza *Spain* ● 29 M5
Iceland *Europe* ▲ 18 (1)C2
Idaho *United States* ▲ 84 C2
IJsselmeer *Netherlands* ➳ 17 J2
Ikaria *Greece* ● 36 H7
Îles Pallisser (Fr. Poly.) *Oceania* ● 73 M7
Ilha de Marajó *Brazil* 97 H4
Illinois *United States* ▲ 86 C2
Iloilo *Philippines* ● 65 G4
Imphal *India* ● 62 H4
Inch'on *South Korea* ● 68 D5
Inderborskiy *Kazakhstan* ● 21 L5
India *Southern Asia* ▲ 62 C4
Indian Ocean *Indian Ocean* 56 K9
Indiana *United States* ▲ 86 C2
Indianapolis *United States* ■ 86 C3
Indonesia *Asia* ▲ 70 C3
Indore *India* ● 62 C4
Indus *Southern Asia* ➳ 41 K4
Inhambane *Mozambique* ● 55 F4
Inn *Europe* ➳ 30 F3
Inner Hebrides *United Kingdom* 14 G5
Innsbruck *Austria* ● 30 G3
Investigator Group *Australia* 74 F6
Ioánnina *Greece* ● 36 C5
Ionian Islands (Iónioi Nísoi) *Greece* 36 B5
Iónioi Nísoi (Ionian Islands) *Europe* 36 B7
Iónioi Nísoi (Ionian Islands) *Greece* 36 B7
Iónioi Pélagos (Ionian Sea) *Europe* 36 B7
Iowa *United States* ▲ 86 B2
Ipoh *Malaysia* ● 70 C2

Ipswich *United Kingdom* ● 15 Q9
Iqaluit *Canada* ■ 81 T4
Iquique *Chile* ● 96 C4
Iráklion *Greece* ● 36 H9
Iran *Middle East* ▲ 41 F3
Iraq *Middle East* ▲ 40 D3
Irbid *Jordan* ● 42 C4
Ireland *Europe* ▲ 15 D8
Irgrz *Kazakhstan* ● 21 N5
Irian Jaya *Indonesia* ● 71 E3
Iringa *Tanzania* ● 53 D8
Irkutsk *Russia* ● 59 J6
Irrawaddy *South East Asia* ➳ 64 B2
Isabela *Ecuador* ● 96 (1)A2
Isafjordur *Iceland* ● 18 B1
Isfahan (Esfahan) *Iran* ● 40 F3
Isla Grande de Tierra del Fuego
   *Chile / Argentina* 98 H9
Islamabad *Pakistan* ■ 41 K3
Islas Baleares (Balearic Isles) *Spain* ● 29 M5
Islas Canarias (Canary Islands) (Sp.)
   *Atlantic Ocean* 46 B3
Islas de los Desventurados *Chile* 98 C6
Islas Galápagos (Galapagos Islands)
   *Ecuador* ● 96 (1)A1
Islas Juan Fernández *Chile* 98 E5
Islas Revillagigedo *Mexico* 92 B5
Isle of Man *United Kingdom* ● 15 H7
Isle of Wight *United Kingdom* ● 15 M11
Isles of Scilly *United Kingdom* ● 15 G12
Isole Eolie o Lipari *Italy* ● 33 J10
Isole Ponziane *Italy* 33 G8
Israel *Middle East* ▲ 42 C4
Istanbul *Turkey* ● 39 C3
Italy *Europe* ▲ 32 E3
Iwaki *Japan* ● 69 L5
Izmir (Smyrna) *Turkey* ● 39 B4
Izmit *Turkey* ● 39 C3
Izu-Shoto *Japan* ● 69 K7

**J**
Jackson *United States* ■ 90 C3
Jacksonville *United States* ● 91 E3
Jaffa (Tel Aviv-Yafo) *Israel* ● 42 B4
Jaipur *India* ● 62 C3
Jakarta *Indonesia* ■ 70 D4
Jakobstad *Finland* ● 18 M5
Jamaica *Caribbean* ▲ 93 J5
Jammu and Kashmir *India* ● 62 C2
Japan *East Asia* ▲ 69 L6
Japan Trench *Pacific Ocean* 69 M5
Java (Jawa) *Indonesia* 70 F4
Java Sea *Asia* 70 E4
Jawa (Java) *Indonesia* 70 F4
Jayapura *Indonesia* ● 71 F3
Jaza'ir Sawakin *Sudan* ● 49 G4
Jebel Toubkal *Morocco* ▲ 46 D2
Jedda (Jiddah) *Saudi Arabia* ● 40 C5
Jefferson City *United States* ■ 86 B3
Jerez de la Frontera *Spain* ● 28 E8
Jersey City *United States* ● 87 F2
Jerusalem (Yerushalayim) *Israel* ■ 42 C5
Jibal al Adhiriyat *Jordan* ▲ 42 C5
Jiddah (Jedda) *Saudi Arabia* ● 40 C5
Jilin *China* ● 67 H2
Jinan *China* ● 66 F3
Jinzhou *China* ● 67 G2
Johannesburg *South Africa* ● 54 D5
John O'Groats *United Kingdom* ● 14 K3
Johor Baharu *Malaysia* ● 70 C2
Jönköping *Sweden* ● 19 G8
Jordan *Middle East* ▲ 42 C6
Joseph Bonaparte Gulf *Australia* 74 E2
Jukka *Finland* ● 18 M5
Juneau *United States* ■ 88 (1)L4
Jura *France / Switzerland* ▲ 27 L7
Jylland *Denmark* ● 19 E8
Jyväskylä *Finland* ● 18 N5

**K**
Kirkkale *Turkey* ● 39 E4
Ka Lae *United States* ● 89 (2)F5
Kabul *Afghanistan* ■ 41 J3
Kabwe *Zambia* ● 52 D2

Kagoshima *Japan* ● 68 F8
Kahramanmaras *Turkey* ● 39 G5
Kaikoura Range *New Zealand* ▲ 77 D6
Kaimanawa Mountains *New Zealand* ▲ 76 E4
Kaiwi Channel *United States* 89 (2)D3
Kajaani *Finland* ● 18 N4
Kalahari Desert *Southern Africa* 54 C4
Kalevala *Russia* ● 18 R4
Kaliningrad *Russia* ● 22 K3
Kampala *Uganda* ■ 53 E3
Kamyshin *Russia* ● 20 K4
Kananga
   *Democratic Republic of Congo* ● 52 C
Kanazawa *Japan* ● 69 J5
Kanchenjunga *Nepal / India* ▲ 62 E3
Kandalaksha *Russia* ● 20 G1
Kangaroo Island *Australia* 75 G7
Kanin Nos *Russia* ● 20 J1
Kankan *Guinea* ● 50 C2
Kanpur *India* ● 62 D3
Kansas *United States* ▲ 86 A3
Kansas City *United States* ● 86 B3
Kara *Russia* ● 21 N1
Kara Sea (Karskoye More) *Russia* 58 L3
Karachi *Pakistan* ● 41 J5
Karadeniz Bogazi (Bosporus) *Turkey* ➳ 39 C3
Karaganda *Kazakhstan* ● 21 Q5
Karakorum *Southern Asia* ▲ 62 C1
Karigasniemi *Sweden* ● 18 N2
Karlovac *Croatia* ● 34 C4
Karlsruhe *Germany* ● 25 D7
Kárpathos *Greece* ● 37 K9
Karskoye More (Kara Sea) *Russia* 58 L3
Kassala *Sudan* ● 49 G4
Katakwi *Uganda* ● 53 E3
Katanga
   *Democratic Republic of Congo* ● 52 C
Kathmandu *Nepal* ■ 62 E3
Katowice *Poland* ● 23 H7
Katsina *Nigeria* ● 51 F2
Kauai Channel *United States* 89 (2)B2
Kauhajoki *Finland* ● 18 M5
Kaunas *Lithuania* ● 19 M9
Kautokeino *Norway* ● 18 M2
Kawasaki *Japan* ● 69 K6
Kayseri *Turkey* ● 39 F4
Kazakhstan *Asia* ▲ 59 L8
Kazan' *Russia* ● 21 K3
Kazhim *Russia* ● 21 L2
Kem *Russia* ● 20 G2
Kemerovo *Russia* ● 59 R6
Kentucky *United States* ▲ 86 C3
Kenya *Central Africa* ▲ 53 F3
Kepulauan Anambas *Indonesia* 70 D2
Kepulauan Batu *Indonesia* 70 B3
Kepulauan Lingga *Indonesia* 70 C2
Kepulauan Maluku *Indonesia* 71 C2
Kepulauan Mentawai *Indonesia* 70 B3
Kepulauan Natuna *Indonesia* 70 D2
Kepulauan Pagai *Indonesia* 70 B3
Kérkira (Corfu) *Greece* ● 36 B5
Kermadec Islands *New Zealand* 73 J8
Kermadec Trench *Oceania* 73 J9
Kerman *Iran* ● 41 G4
Kharagpur *India* ● 62 E4
Kharkiv *Ukraine* ● 20 H4
Kharabali *Kazakhstan* ● 21 K5
Kharkov *Ukraine* ● 20 H4
Khartoum (El Khartum) *Sudan* ■ 49 F4
Khaskovo *Bulgaria* ● 35 N8
Khíos *Greece* ● 36 H6
Kiel *Germany* ● 24 F6
Kielce *Poland* ● 23 K7
Kiev (Kyyiv) *Ukraine* ■ 20 G4
Kigali *Rwanda* ■ 52 E7
Kikwit *Democratic Republic of Congo* ● 52 B5
Kilimanjaro *Tanzania* ▲ 53 F4
Kilkenny *Ireland* ● 15 E9
Kimberley Plateau *Australia* 74 E3
King Leopold Ranges *Australia* ▲ 74 D3
King's Lynn *United Kingdom* ● 16 D2
Kingston *Jamaica* ■ 93 J5
Kingston upon Hull *United Kingdom* ● 15 N8

shasa
Democratic Republic of Congo 51 H5
bati Oceania 73 J6
›vsk Russia 18 S3
ına Sweden 18 L3
maayo Somalia 53 G4
umu Kenya 53 E3
ı-Kyushu Japan 68 F7
ıira Greece 36 E8
ipeda Lithuania 19 L9
›e Japan 68 H6
›enhavn (Copenhagen) Denmark 19 F9
›lenz Germany 17 L4
ıchetav Kazakhstan 21 P4
n (Cologne) Germany 25 B6
motiní Greece 36 H3
nsomol'sk-na-Amure Russia 61 P6
ıgolo
Democratic Republic of Congo 52 D5
ıgur Shan China 59 P10
ıya Turkey 39 E5
ea Strait (Taehan-Haehyop)
South Korea / Japan 68 D7
ea Strait (Tsushima-Kaikyo)
South Korea / Japan 68 D7
la China 59 R9
›oglu Daglari Turkey 39 D3
trijk Belgium 16 G4
s Greece 37 K8
sice Slovakia 23 L9
slan Russia 21 K2
sovska/Mitrovica Yugoslavia 34 H7
stroma Russia 20 J3
wloon China 66 E6
záni Greece 36 D4
ıków Poland 23 J7
ısnodar Russia 20 H5
ısnosel'kup Russia 21 S1
ısnoyarsk Russia 59 S6
ıfeld Germany 25 B5
stiansand Norway 19 D7
stiansund Norway 18 D5
i (Crete) Greece 36 G9
ıng Thep (Bangkok) Thailand 64 C4
ala Lumpur Malaysia 70 C2
hmo Finland 18 Q4
mamoto Japan 68 F7
manovo Macedonia 36 D2
masi Ghana 50 D3
nming China 66 C5
pang Indonesia 71 B5
ril Islands (Kuril'skije Ostrova)
Russia 61 S8
ril Trench Pacific Ocean 69 P2
il'skije Ostrova (Kuril Islands)
Russia 61 S8
sk Russia 20 H4
stanay Kazakhstan 59 L7
wait Middle East 43 B2
wait (Al Kuwayt) Kuwait 43 C2
zomen Russia 20 H1
angju South Korea 68 D6
klades (Cyclades) Greece 36 G7
oto Japan 68 H6
gyzstan Asia 59 N9
ıshu Japan 68 F7
yiv (Kiev) Ukraine 20 G4
yl-Orda Kazakhstan 21 P6



Coruña Spain 28 B1
Manche / English Channel
United Kingdom / France 15 L11
Paz Bolivia 96 D7
Pérouse Strait Russia / Japan 67 L1
›e (Elbe)
Germany / Czech Republic 25 K6
›rador Sea North America 81 V4
: Léman (Lake Geneva)
Switzerland / France 30 B4
: Tchad (Lake Chad)
Chad / Cameroon 48 B5
ccadive Islands (Ind.) Arabian Sea 63 B6



Ladozhskoye Ozero (Lake Ladoga)
Russia 20 G2
Lago de Nicaragua Nicaragua 93 G6
Lago Titicaca Bolivia / Peru 96 D7
Lagos Nigeria 51 E3
Laguna Mar Chiquita Argentina 98 J5
Lahore Pakistan 41 K3
Laï Chad 48 C6
Lake Baikal (Ozero Baykal) Russia 60 H6
Lake Balkhash (Ozero Balkhash)
Kazakhstan 59 P8
Lake Barlee Australia 74 C5
Lake Chad (Lac Tchad)
Chad / Cameroon 48 B5
Lake Disappointment Australia 74 D4
Lake Ellesmere New Zealand 77 D6
Lake Erie North America 87 D2
Lake Eyre North Australia 75 G5
Lake Eyre South Australia 75 G5
Lake Gairdner Australia 75 G6
Lake Geneva (Lac Léman)
Switzerland / France 30 B4
Lake Huron United States / Canada 86 D2
Lake Khanka (Ozero Khanka)
China / Russia 67 J1
Lake Ladoga (Ladozhskoye Ozero)
Russia 20 G2
Lake Mackay Australia 74 E4
Lake Macleod Australia 74 B4
Lake Malawi (Lake Nyasa)
Malawi / Mozambique 55 E2
Lake Michigan United States 86 C2
Lake Nasser Egypt 49 F3
Lake Nyasa (Lake Malawi)
Malawi / Mozambique 55 E2
Lake Onega (Ozero Onezhskoye)
Russia 20 H2
Lake Ontario North America 87 E2
Lake Peipus (Pskovskoye Ozero)
Russia 20 F3
Lake Superior United States / Canada 86 C1
Lake Tanganyika Central Africa 52 D5
Lake Te Anau New Zealand 77 A7
Lake Tiberias (Yam Kinneret) Israel 42 C4
Lake Torrens Australia 75 G6
Lake Victoria Central Africa 53 E4
Lake Volta Ghana 50 D3
Lake Winnipeg Canada 80 M6
Lamia Greece 36 E6
Lamu Kenya 53 G4
Land's End United Kingdom 15 H11
Lansing United States 86 D2
Lanzhou China 66 C3
Laos South East Asia 64 C2
Laptev Sea (More Laptevykh) Russia 60 L2
Lar Iran 43 F3
Lárisa Greece 36 E5
Las Palmas de Gran Canaria
Canary Islands 46 B3
Las Vegas United States 88 C1
Latvia Europe 19 M8
Lau Group (Fiji) Oceania 73 J7
Lausanne Switzerland 30 B4
Lavrentiya Russia 61 Z3
Le Havre France 26 F4
Le Mans France 26 F5
Lebanon Middle East 42 C3
Leeds United Kingdom 15 M8
Leeward Islands Caribbean 93 M5
Leganés Spain 28 F4
Leghorn (Livorno) Italy 32 E5
Leicester United Kingdom 16 B2
Leipzig Germany 25 H5
Lelystad Netherlands 17 J2
Lemesós (Limassol) Cyprus 37 R10
Lena Russia 60 M4
León Spain 28 E2
Lesbos (Lésvos) Greece 36 J5
Leskovac Yugoslavia 34 J7
Lesotho Southern Africa 54 D5
Lesser Antilles Caribbean 93 K6
Lesser Sunda Islands Indonesia 70 F4
Lésvos (Lesbos) Greece 36 J5
Levkósia (Nicosia) Cyprus 37 R9



Lexington United States 91 E2
Liberia West Africa 50 C3
Libreville Gabon 51 F4
Libya North Africa 48 C2
Libyan Desert (As Sahra' al Libiyah)
Libya 48 D2
Liechtenstein Europe 30 E3
Liège Belgium 17 J4
Liepaja Latvia 19 L8
Ligurian Sea Europe 32 C5
Likasi Democratic Republic of Congo 52 D6
Lille France 26 H3
Lillehammer Norway 19 F6
Lilongwe Malawi 55 E2
Lima Peru 96 B6
Limassol (Lemesós) Cyprus 37 R10
Limerick Ireland 15 E9
Limoges France 27 G8
Limpopo Southern Africa 55 E4
Lincoln United States 85 G2
Line Islands (Kiribati) Oceania 73 L6
Linköping Sweden 19 H7
Linz Austria 31 K2
Lisboa (Lisbon) Portugal 28 A6
Lisbon (Lisboa) Portugal 28 A6
Lithuania Europe 19 M9
Little Rock United States 90 C3
Liverpool United Kingdom 15 K8
Livingstone Zambia 54 D3
Livorno (Leghorn) Italy 32 E5
Lizard Point United Kingdom 15 H12
Ljubljana Slovenia 34 B3
Lobito Angola 52 A6
Lódz Poland 22 J6
Lofoten Norway 18 G2
Loire France 26 D6
Lomé Togo 50 E3
London Canada 87 D2
London United Kingdom 15 N10
Londonderry United Kingdom 14 F6
Long Beach United States 88 C2
Long Island United States 87 F2
Los Angeles United States 88 C2
Lough Neagh United Kingdom 15 G7
Louisiana United States 90 C3
Lovozero Russia 18 T2
Luanda Angola 52 A5
Lubbock United States 89 F2
Lübeck Germany 24 F3
Lublin Poland 22 M6
Lubumbashi
Democratic Republic of Congo 52 D6
Lucknow India 62 D3
Lüderitz Namibia 54 B5
Ludwigshafen Germany 17 M5
Lulea Sweden 18 M4
Luoyang China 66 E3
Lusaka Zambia 54 D3
Luton United Kingdom 16 C3
Luxembourg Europe 17 J5
Luxembourg Luxembourg 17 K5
Luzon Philippines 65 G3
Lycksele Sweden 18 K4
Lyon France 27 K8


## M


Ma'an Jordan 42 C6
Maas Central Europe 24 B5
Maastricht Netherlands 17 J4
Macau Macau (Portugal) 66 E6
Macau (Portugal) South East Asia 66 E6
Macdonnell Ranges Australia 74 F4
Macedonia Europe 36 C3
Maceió Brazil 97 K5
Macgillycuddy's Reeks Ireland 15 C10
Mackay Australia 75 J4
Mackenzie United States 88 (1)M2
Mackenzie Mountains Canada 88 (1)K3
Macon United States 91 E3
Madagascar Southern Africa 55 G4
Madama Niger 47 H4
Madeira Portugal 46 B2
Madison United States 86 C2
Madrid Spain 28 G4

Madurai *India* 63 C7
Magadan *Russia* 61 S5
Magdeburg *Germany* 24 G4
Magnitogorsk *Russia* 21 M4
Mahia Peninsula *New Zealand* 76 F4
Maidstone *United Kingdom* 16 D3
Maiduguri *Nigeria* 51 G2
Main *Germany* 25 D6
Maine *United States* 87 G1
Mainz *Germany* 17 M5
Majerten *Somalia* 53 H2
Makassar Strait *Indonesia* 71 A3
Makhachkala *Russia* 39 M2
Makkah (Mecca) *Saudi Arabia* 40 D5
Malabo *Equatorial Guinea* 51 F4
Málaga *Spain* 28 F8
Malang *Malaysia* 70 C4
Malatya *Turkey* 39 H4
Malawi *Southern Africa* 55 E2
Malaysia *Asia* 70 C2
Maldives *Indian Ocean* 63 B8
Mali *West Africa* 46 E5
Malin Head *Ireland* 14 F6
Mallorca *Spain* 29 P5
Malmö *Sweden* 19 G9
Malpelo Eagle 33 J13
Malta Channel *Italy* 33 J12
Malta *Southern Europe* 33 J11
Manado *Indonesia* 71 B2
Managua *Nicaragua* 93 G6
Manama (Al Manamah) *Bahrain* 43 D3
Manaus *Brazil* 96 E4
Manchester *United Kingdom* 15 L8
Mandalay *Myanmar (Burma)* 64 B2
Manila *Philippines* 65 G4
Manokwari *Indonesia* 71 D3
Maputo *Mozambique* 55 E5
Mar Cantábrico *Spain* 28 D1
Mar del Plata *Argentina* 99 K6
Maracaibo *Venezuela* 96 C1
Maracay *Venezuela* 96 E1
Mare Tirreno (Tyrrhenian Sea) *Italy* 33 G9
Maribor *Slovenia* 34 C3
Marica *Bulgaria* 35 N7
Marmara Denizi (Sea of Marmara)
 *Turkey* 39 B3
Maroua *Cameroon* 51 G2
Marquesas Islands (Fr. Poly.) *Oceania* 73 N6
Marseille *France* 27 L10
Marshall Islands *Oceania* 72 G4
Martinique (Fr.) *Caribbean* 93 M6
Maryland *United States* 87 E3
Maseru *Lesotho* 54 D5
Mashhad *Iran* 41 G2
Masqat (Muscat) *Oman* 43 H5
Massachusetts *United States* 87 F2
Massif Central *France* 27 K8
Matadi *Democratic Republic of Congo* 52 A5
Mauna Kea *United States* 89 (2)F4
Mauritania *West Africa* 46 C5
Mauritius *Indian Ocean* 55 (1)B2
Mayotte (France) *Indian Ocean* 55 H2
Mbabane *Swaziland* 55 E5
Mbandaka
 *Democratic Republic of Congo* 52 B4
Mbeya *Tanzania* 53 E5
Mbuji-Mayi
 *Democratic Republic of Congo* 52 B4
Mecca (Makkah) *Saudi Arabia* 40 D5
Mecklenburger Bucht *Germany* 24 G2
Medan *Indonesia* 70 B2
Medellín *Colombia* 96 B2
Medina (Al Madinah) *Saudi Arabia* 40 C5
Mediterranean Sea *Europe* 12 E4
Mekong *South East Asia* 64 F5
Melaka *Malaysia* 72 F5
Melbourne *Australia* 75 H7
Melilla *Spain* 28 H9
Memphis *United States* 90 C2
Menorca *Spain* 29 Q5
Mercury Islands *New Zealand* 76 B3
Mergui Archipelago *Myanmar (Burma)* 64 B4

Merlitopol' *Ukraine* 20 H5
Messina *Sicily* 33 K10
Metz *France* 17 K5
Mexicali *Mexico* 92 A2
Mexico *Central America* 92 C4
Mexico City (Ciudad de México)
 *Mexico* 92 D5
Miami *United States* 91 E4
Miass *Russia* 21 M3
Michigan *United States* 86 C2
Micronesia *Oceania* 72 F4
Mid-Atlantic Ridge *Atlantic Ocean* 94 G2
Middlesbrough *United Kingdom* 15 M7
Milan (Milano) *Italy* 32 D3
Milano (Milan) *Italy* 32 D3
Milwaukee *United States* 86 C2
Mindanao *Philippines* 65 H5
Mindoro *Philippines* 65 G4
Mindoro Strait *Philippines* 65 G4
Minneapolis *United States* 86 B1
Minnesota *United States* 86 B1
Minsk *Belarus* 20 F4
Mírtóon Pélagos *Greece* 36 F7
Miskolc *Hungary* 23 K9
Misratah *Libya* 48 C1
Mississippi *United States* 90 C3
Mississippi *United States* 90 C2
Mississippi Delta *United States* 90 D4
Missouri *United States* 90 C2
Missouri River *United States* 90 C2
Mobile *United States* 90 D3
Modena *Italy* 32 E4
Mogadishu (Muqdisho) *Somalia* 53 H3
Mojave Desert *United States* 88 C2
Moldova *Europe* 35 R2
Molucca Sea *Indonesia* 71 C3
Mombasa *Kenya* 53 F4
Monaco *Europe* 32 C7
Mönchengladbach *Germany* 25 B5
Mongolia *Asia* 60 H7
Monrovia *Liberia* 50 B3
Mons *Belgium* 17 G4
Mont Blanc *France / Italy* 30 B5
Montana *United States* 85 D1
Monte Carlo *Monaco* 32 B5
Monte Perdido *Spain* 29 L2
Monterrey *Mexico* 92 E3
Montevideo *Uruguay* 99 K5
Montgomery *United States* 90 D3
Montpelier *United States* 87 F2
Montpellier *France* 27 L10
Montréal *Canada* 81 S7
Monts de la Medjerda
 *Tunisia / Algeria* 33 C12
Monts Mitumba
 *Democratic Republic of Congo* 52 D4
Montserrat (U.K.) *Caribbean* 93 M5
Moray Firth *United Kingdom* 14 K4
More Laptevykh (Laptev Sea) *Russia* 60 L2
Morocco *North Africa* 46 D2
Moroni *Comoros* 55 G2
Moscow (Moskva) *Russia* 20 H3
Moskva (Moscow) *Russia* 20 H3
Mostaganem *Algeria* 29 T9
Mosul (Al Mawsil) *Iraq* 40 D2
Moulmein *Myanmar (Burma)* 64 B2
Mount Apo *Philippines* 65 H5
Mount Ararat (Büyük Ağrı Dağı)
 *Turkey* 39 L4
Mount Cook *New Zealand* 77 C6
Mount Everest *Nepal / China* 62 E3
Mount Kenya / Kirinyaga *Kenya* 53 F4
Mount Kosciusko *Australia* 75 J7
Mount McKinley *United States* 88 (1)G3
Mount Troodos (Olympus) *Cyprus* 37 Q10
Mount Whitney *United States* 84 C3
Mourne Mountains *United Kingdom* 15 G7
Mouths of the Niger *Atlantic Ocean* 51 F4
Moyale *Ethiopia / Kenya* 53 F3
Mozambique *Southern Africa* 54 E3
Mozambique Channel *Mozambique* 45 G8
Mtwara *Tanzania* 55 C3
Mulhouse *France* 30 C3

Mumbai / Bombay *India* 63 B5
München (Munich) *Germany* 25 G8
Munich (München) *Germany* 25 G8
Münster *Germany* 24 C5
Muqdisho (Mogadishu) *Somalia* 53 H3
Murcia *Spain* 29 J7
Murmansk *Russia* 58 E4
Murray River *Australia* 75 G6
Muscat (Masqat) *Oman* 43 H5
Musgrave Ranges *Australia* 74 F5
Mwanza *Tanzania* 53 E4
Myanmar (Burma) *Southern Asia* 64 A2

# N

Naberezhnyye Chelny *Russia* 21 L3
Nagasaki *Japan* 68 F7
Nagoya *Japan* 69 J6
Nagpur *India* 62 C4
Nahr an Nîl (Nile) *Egypt / Sudan* 49 F2
Nairobi *Kenya* 53 F4
Namangan *Uzbekistan* 59 N9
Namib Desert *Namibia* 54 A3
Namibe *Angola* 54 A3
Namibia *Southern Africa* 54 B4
Nampula *Mozambique* 55 F3
Namsos *Norway* 18 F4
Namur *Belgium* 17 H4
Nan Hai (South China Sea) *China* 65 E3
Nanchang *China* 66 F3
Nancy *France* 26 M5
Nanjing *China* 66 F2
Nantes *France* 26 D6
Narvik *Norway* 18 J2
Nashville *United States* 90 D2
Nassau *Bahamas* 91 F4
Natal *Brazil* 97 K5
Natitingou *Benin* 50 E2
Nauru *Oceania* 72 G6
Nauru (Nauru) *Oceania* 72 G6
Nazca Ridge *Pacific Ocean* 98 E3
N'Djamena *Chad* 52 C4
Ndola *Zambia* 54 D2
Nebraska *United States* 85 F2
Neder-Rijn *Netherlands* 17 J3
Negev *Israel* 42 B5
Nelson *New Zealand* 77 D5
Nepal *Southern Asia* 62 D3
Neskaupstadur *Iceland* 18 (1)G2
Netherlands Antilles *Caribbean* 93 L6
Nevada *United States* 84 C3
New Brunswick *Canada* 81 T7
New Caledonia (Fr.) *Oceania* 72 G7
New Delhi *India* 62 C3
New Guinea
 *South East Asia / Oceania* 71
New Hampshire *United States* 87 F2
New Jersey *United States* 87 F3
New Mexico *United States* 89 E2
New Orleans *United States* 90 C3
New Plymouth *New Zealand* 76 E4
New Providence *Bahamas* 91 F4
New Siberian Islands (Novosibirskiye Ostrova)
 *Russia* 61 N2
New South Wales *Australia* 75 H6
New York *United States* 87 F2
New York *United States* 87 F2
New Zealand *New Zealand* 76 B4
Newark *United States* 87 F2
Newcastle *Australia* 75 K6
Newcastle upon Tyne *United Kingdom* 14
Newfoundland *Canada* 81 V7
Newfoundland and Labrador *Canada* 81 U0
Newport *United Kingdom* 15 L10
Ngaoundéré *Cameroon* 51 G3
Nha Trang *Vietnam* 64 D4
Niagara Falls *United States / Canada* 87 E2
Niamey *Niger* 51 E2
Nicaragua *Central America* 93 G6
Nice *France* 27 N10
Nicobar Islands *India* 63 F7
Nicosia (Levkósia) *Cyprus* 37 R9

er West Africa ◪ 51 F3
…ria West Africa ▣ 51 F3
…ata Japan ◉ 69 K5
…egen Netherlands ◉ 17 J3
… (Nahr an Nil) Africa ◪ 49 F2
…nes France ◉ 27 K10
… Degree Channel Arabian Sea ⬜ 63 B7
…dgo China ▣ 67 G5
… Yugoslavia ◪ 34 J6
…e (N.Z.) Oceania ⬜ 73 K8
…hnevartovsk Russia ◉ 58 P5
…hniy Novgorod Russia ◉ 20 J3
…hniy Tagil Russia ◉ 58 L6
…angsamba Cameroon ◉ 51 G3
…drfriese Inseln Germany ◪ 24 C2
…dckapp Norway ◉ 18 P1
…folk United States ◉ 91 F2
…il'sk Russia ◉ 58 R4
…rköping Sweden ◉ 19 J7
…h Cape New Zealand ◉ 76 D2
…h Carolina United States ◉ 91 E2
…h Channel
United Kingdom / Ireland ⬜ 15 H7
…h Dakota United States ◉ 85 F1
…h East Pacific Basin Oceania ⬜ 73 M4
…h Island New Zealand ⬜ 76 D3
…h Korea South East Asia ▣ 68 A4
…h Sea Europe ⬜ 14 Q3
…h Siberian Plain (Severo-Sibirskaya
…menndst) Russia ⬜ 59 K3
…hni Taranaki Bight New Zealand ⬜ 76 E4
…h West Highlands
United Kingdom ⬜ 14 H5
…h Yorks Moors United Kingdom ⬜ 15 M7
…thampton United Kingdom ◉ 16 C2
…hern Ireland United Kingdom ▣ 15 F7
…hern Mariana Islands (U.S.)
Oceania ⬜ 72 F4
…hern Sporades (Vóries Sporádes)
Greece ⬜ 36 F6
…hern Territory Australia ◪ 74 F4
…west Christmas Island Ridge
Oceania ⬜ 73 K4
…thwest Territories Canada ◪ 80 J4
…way Europe ▣ 18 E5
…wegian Sea Norway ⬜ 18 B4
…wich United Kingdom ◉ 15 Q9
…tingham United Kingdom ◉ 15 M9
…uádhibou Western Sahara ◉ 46 B4
…uakchott Mauritania ▣ 46 B5
…ra Scotia Canada ◪ 81 U8
…vaya Zemlya Russia ⬜ 58 J3
…iri Sad Yugoslavia ⬜ 34 J4
…vokazalinsk Kazakhstan ◉ 21 N5
…okuzmetsk Russia ◉ 59 R7
…vorossiysk Russia ◉ 20 H6
…oshakhtinsk Russia ◉ 20 H5
…osibirsk Russia ◉ 59 Q6
…osibirskaya Ostrova (New Siberian Islands)
Russia ⬜ 61 P1
…bian Desert (As Sahra' an Nubiyah)
Sudan ◪ 49 F3
…arbor Plain Australia ⬜ 74 E6
…enberg Germany ◉ 25 G7
…ala Sudan ◉ 48 D5
…brekoré Guinea ◉ 50 C3

…hu United States ⬜ 89 (2)D2
…kland United States ◉ 84 B3
… Russia ⬜ 58 Q6
…thausen Germany ◉ 24 B5
…ava Croatia ◉ 34 C5
…da Norway ◉ 19 D6
…ense Denmark ◉ 19 E9
…er Germany / Poland ◪ 24 K4
…essa Ukraine ◉ 20 G5
…enné Côte D'Ivoire ◉ 50 C3
… a Poland ◪ 22 D5
…o United States ◉ 86 D2
…io River United States ◉ 87 D3
…mayo Indonesia ◉ 71 E4
…ayama Japan ◉ 68 H6

Oklahoma United States ◪ 90 B2
Oklahoma City United States ▣ 90 B2
Oktyabr'skoye Russia ◉ 58 M5
Oldenburg Germany ◉ 17 M1
Olbmos (Olympus) Greece ⬜ 36 E4
Olomouc Czech Republic ◉ 23 G8
Olongapo Philippines ◉ 65 F4
Olsztyn Poland ◉ 22 K4
Olympia United States ▣ 84 B1
Olympus (Olimbos) Greece ⬜ 36 E4
Olympus (Mount Troodos) Cyprus ⬜ 37 Q10
Omaha United States ◉ 85 G2
Oman Middle East ▣ 41 H6
Omsk Russia ◉ 59 N6
Ontario Canada ◪ 81 R7
Oostende (Ostend) Belgium ◉ 16 F3
Oporto (Porto) Portugal ◉ 28 B3
Oradea Romania ◉ 34 H2
Oradea Romania ◉ 34 J2
Oran Algeria ◉ 47 E1
Orange/Oranje Southern Africa ⬜ 54 B5
Orango Guinea-Bissau ⬜ 50 A2
Örebro Sweden ◉ 19 H7
Oregon United States ◪ 84 B2
Orenburg Russia ◉ 59 K7
Orinoco South America ⬜ 96 D2
Orkney Islands United Kingdom ⬜ 14 L2
Orumiyeh Iran ◉ 39 L5
Osaka Japan ◉ 68 H6
Osh Kyrgyzstan ◉ 59 N9
Osijek Croatia ◉ 34 F4
Oslo Norway ▣ 19 F7
Osnabrück Germany ◉ 17 M2
Ost-Alpen Austria ⬜ 34 B1
Ostend (Oostende) Belgium ◉ 16 F3
Ostfriesische Inseln Germany ⬜ 24 B3
Ostrava Czech Republic ◉ 23 H8
Ostrova Sakhalin Russia ⬜ 61 Q6
Ottawa Canada ▣ 87 F2
Ouagadougou Burkina Faso ▣ 50 D2
Outer Hebrides United Kingdom ⬜ 14 F4
Ovando Congo ◉ 52 B4
Oxford United Kingdom ◉ 15 M10
Ozero Balkhash (Lake Balkhash)
Kazakhstan ⬜ 59 P8
Ozero Baykal (Lake Baikal) Russia ⬜ 60 M6
Ozero Khanka (Lake Khanka)
China / Russia ⬜ 67 J1
Ozero Onezhskoye (Lake Onega)
Russia ⬜ 20 H2
Ozero Sevan Armenia ⬜ 39 L3

**P**

Pacific Ocean Pacific Ocean ⬜ 57 U9
Padang Indonesia ◉ 70 C3
Paderborn Germany ◉ 17 M3
Padova Italy ◉ 32 F3
Pakistan Southern Asia ▣ 41 J4
Palagruza Croatia ⬜ 34 D7
Palau (Palau) Oceania ⬜ 72 D5
Palawan Philippines ⬜ 65 F5
Palembang Indonesia ◉ 70 C3
Palermo Sicily ◉ 33 H10
Palma Spain ◉ 29 H6
Palmerston North New Zealand ◉ 76 E5
Pampas Argentina ⬜ 98 H6
Pamplona Spain ◉ 29 J2
Panama Central America ▣ 93 H7
Panama Canal (Canal de Panama)
Panama ⬜ 93 J7
Panama City Panama ▣ 93 J7
Papenburg Germany ◉ 17 M1
Papua New Guinea Oceania ▣ 72 E6
Paraguay South America ▣ 98 J3
Paraguay South America ⬜ 99 K3
Paramaribo Surinam ▣ 97 F2
Paraná Argentina ◉ 98 J5
Paraná South America ⬜ 98 K4
Parc National de la Salonga
Democratic Republic of Congo ⬜ 52 C4
Paris France ▣ 26 H6
Parma Italy ◉ 32 E4
Patagonia Argentina ⬜ 98 G7

Patna India ◉ 62 E3
Pátrai Greece ◉ 36 D6
Pavlodar Kazakhstan ◉ 59 P7
Pazardzhik Bulgaria ◉ 35 M7
Pécs Hungary ◉ 23 H11
Pegasus Bay New Zealand ⬜ 77 D6
Pegu Myanmar (Burma) ◉ 64 B3
Peninsular Malaysia Malaysia ⬜ 70 C1
Pennines United Kingdom ⬜ 15 L7
Pennsylvania United States ◪ 87 E2
Pentland Firth United Kingdom ⬜ 14 K3
Peoria United States ◉ 86 C2
Perm Russia ◉ 21 K4
Pernik Bulgaria ◉ 35 L7
Perpignan France ◉ 27 J11
Perth Australia ▣ 74 C6
Peru South America ▣ 96 B5
Peru-Chile Trench Pacific Ocean ⬜ 94 D5
Perugia Italy ◉ 32 G5
Peter I. Øy Antarctica ⬜ 100 (2)JJ3
Petropavlovsk Kazakhstan ◉ 21 P4
Petropavlovsk-Kamchatskiy Russia ◉ 61 T6
Petrozavodsk Russia ◉ 20 G2
Philadelphia United States ◉ 87 E2
Philippines South East Asia ▣ 65 G5
Phnom Penh Cambodia ▣ 64 D4
Phoenix United States ▣ 88 D2
Phoenix Islands (Kiribati) Oceania ⬜ 73 J6
Pico de Almanzor Spain ⬜ 28 E4
Pierre United States ▣ 85 F2
Pindos Oros Greece ⬜ 36 D5
Pingxiang China ◉ 66 E5
Piréas Greece ◉ 36 E7
Pisa Italy ◉ 32 E5
Pitcairn Islands (U.K.) Oceania ⬜ 73 P8
Pittsburgh United States ◉ 87 E2
Piura Peru ◉ 96 A5
Planalto do Brasil (Brazilian Highlands)
Brazil ⬜ 97 J7
Planalto do Mato Grosso Brazil ⬜ 97 F6
Platte River United States ⬜ 85 F2
Ploiesti Romania ◉ 35 P5
Plovdiv Bulgaria ◉ 35 M7
Plymouth United Kingdom ◉ 16 H6
Plzen Czech Republic ◉ 23 C8
Po Italy ⬜ 32 E4
Podgorica Yugoslavia ◉ 34 G7
Poggibonsi Italy ◉ 30 G7
Pointe de Barfleur France ⬜ 16 B5
Pointe Noire Congo ◉ 51 G5
Pojezierze Wielkopolsko-Kujawskie
Poland ⬜ 22 G5
Poland Europe ▣ 22 F5
Polynesia Oceania ⬜ 73 J6
Ponoy Russia ◉ 20 J1
Pontianak Indonesia ◉ 70 D3
Poona (Pune) India ◉ 63 B5
Port Elizabeth South Africa ◉ 54 D6
Port Gentil Gabon ◉ 51 F5
Port Harcourt Nigeria ◉ 51 F4
Port of Spain Trinidad and Tobago ▣ 93 M6
Port Said (Bûr Sa'îd) Egypt ◉ 49 F1
Port Sudan (Bur Sudan) Sudan ◉ 49 G4
Port-au-Prince Haiti ▣ 93 K5
Port-Louis Mauritius ▣ 55 (1)B2
Portland United States ◉ 84 B1
Pôrto Alegre Brazil ◉ 99 K5
Porto (Oporto) Portugal ◉ 28 B3
Porto-Novo Benin ▣ 51 E3
Portsmouth United Kingdom ◉ 16 B4
Portugal Europe ▣ 28 B6
Potsdam Germany ◉ 24 F4
Poznan Poland ◉ 22 F5
Prague (Praha) Czech Republic ▣ 23 D7
Praha (Prague) Czech Republic ▣ 23 D7
Praia Cape Verde ▣ 50 A5
Prato Italy ◉ 32 F5
Pretoria South Africa ▣ 54 D5
Pribilov Islands Russia ⬜ 89 (1)D4
Prilep Macedonia ◉ 34 J8
Prince Edward Island Canada ◪ 81 U7
Prince Edward Island Canada ◪ 81 U7
Pristina Yugoslavia ◉ 34 J7
Probilov Islands United States ⬜ 88 (1)D4

Providence *United States* ⊙ 87 F2
Pskov *Russia* ⊙ 20 F3
Pskovskoye Ozero (Lake Peipus)
*Russia* ◪ 20 F3
Pudasjärvi *Finland* ⊙ 18 P4
Puebla de Zaragoza *Mexico* ⊙ 92 E5
Pueblo *United States* ⊙ 85 F3
Puerto Rico (U.S.) *Caribbean* ⊙ 93 L5
Pulau Timor *Indonesia* ◪ 71 B4
Pune (Poona) *India* ⊙ 63 B5
Punta Arenas *Chile* ⊙ 98 G9
Punta Gallinas *Colombia* ⊙ 96 C1
Punta Negra *Peru* ⊙ 96 A5
Pusan *South Korea* ⊙ 68 E6
P'yongyang *North Korea* ⊛ 68 C4
Pyrénées / Pirineos *France / Spain* ▲ 29 K2

**Q**
Qatar *Middle East* ▣ 43 D4
Qingdao *China* ⊙ 67 G3
Qiqihar *China* ⊙ 67 G1
Qogir Feng / K2 *Pakistan / India* ▲ 62 C1
Quardho *Somalia* ⊙ 53 H2
Québec *Canada* ▣ 81 S6
Québec *Canada* ⊙ 81 S7
Queen Charlotte Islands *Canada* ◪ 80 E6
Queen Elizabeth Islands *Canada* ◪ 80 J2
Queensland *Australia* ▣ 75 H4
Queenstown *New Zealand* ⊙ 77 B7
Quelimane *Mozambique* ⊙ 54 E3
Quelpart I. (Cheju-Do) *South Korea* ◪ 68 D7
Quemoy *Taiwan* ◪ 65 F2
Quezon City *Philippines* ⊙ 65 G4
Quito *Ecuador* ⊛ 96 B3

**R**
Ra's al Hadd *Oman* ▷ 41 H5
Rabat *Morocco* ⊛ 46 D2
Radom *Poland* ⊙ 22 L4
Raleigh *United States* ⊛ 91 F2
Ralik Chain (Marshall Is.) *Oceania* ◪ 72 G5
Ramapo Deep *Pacific Ocean* ◪ 69 M8
Rangoon (Yangon) *Myanmar (Burma)* ⊛ 64 B3
Ras Dashen *Ethiopia* ▲ 49 F5
Rasht *Iran* ⊙ 39 N5
Rat Islands *United States* ◪ 88 (3)B1
Ratak Chain (marshall Is.) *Oceania* ◪ 72 H4
Ravenna *Italy* ⊙ 31 H6
Reading *United Kingdom* ⊙ 15 N10
Recife *Brazil* ⊙ 97 L6
Red Sea *Middle East* ◪ 49 G2
Regensburg *Germany* ⊙ 31 H7
Reggane *Algeria* ⊙ 47 F3
Reggio di Calabria *Italy* ⊙ 33 K10
Regina *Canada* ⊛ 80 M6
Reims *France* ⊙ 26 K4
Reno *United States* ⊙ 84 C3
Repvåg *Norway* ⊙ 18 N1
Resistencia *Argentina* ⊙ 98 K4
Réunion (France) *Southern Africa* ◪ 55 (1)B2
Reykjavik *Iceland* ⊛ 18 (1)B2
Rhein / Rhin (Rhine) *Central Europe* ◪ 24 B5
Rheinisches Schiefergebirge *Germany* ▲ 17 K4
Rhine (Rhein / Rhin) *Central Europe* ◪ 24 B5
Rhode Island *United States* ▣ 87 F2
Rhodes (Ródhos) *Greece* ◪ 37 L8
Rhône / Rhône *Switzerland / France* ◪ 30 C4
Ribnica *Slovenia* ⊙ 34 B4
Ribeirão Preto *Brazil* ⊙ 91 F2
Riga *Latvia* ⊛ 19 N8
Rijeka *Croatia* ⊙ 34 B4
Rimini *Italy* ⊙ 31 H6
Rio Bravo del Norte *Mexico* ◪ 92 D3
Rio de Janeiro *Brazil* ⊙ 99 N3
Rio de la Plata *South America* ◪ 99 K5
Rio Grande *United States* ◪ 89 F3
Rio Negro *South America* ◪ 96 E4
River Cess *Liberia* ⊙ 50 C3
Riyadh (Ar Riyad) *Saudi Arabia* ⊛ 40 E5
Rochester *United States* ⊙ 87 E2
Rockall Bank *United Kingdom* ◪ 14 C4
Rockford *United States* ⊙ 86 C2

Rocky Mountains
*United States / Canada* ▲ 80 E5
Ródhos (Rhodes) *Greece* ◪ 37 L8
Roma (Rome) *Italy* ⊛ 32 G7
Romania *Europe* ▣ 35 L4
Roma (Roma) *Italy* ⊛ 32 G7
Ronne Ice Shelf *Antarctica* ◪ 100 (2)LL1
Rosemary Bank *United Kingdom* ◪ 14 C2
Roseries Reservoir *Sudan* ◪ 49 F5
Ross Ice Shelf *Antarctica* ◪ 100 (2)22
Ross Sea *Antarctica* ◪ 100 (2)22
Rostock *Germany* ⊙ 24 H2
Rostov-na-Donu *Russia* ⊙ 20 H5
Rotterdam *Netherlands* ⊙ 17 H3
Roubaix *France* ⊙ 16 G4
Rouen *France* ⊙ 26 H3
Rub al Khali *Saudi Arabia* ◪ 40 E6
Rudnyy *Kazakhstan* ⊙ 21 N4
Ruhr *Germany* ◪ 25 B5
Rumbek *Sudan* ⊙ 52 D2
Rundu *Namibia* ⊙ 54 B3
Ruse *Bulgaria* ⊙ 35 N6
Russia *Asia* ▣ 58 M6
Russia *Europe* ▣ 22 K3
Ruvuma/Rovuma *Central Africa* ◪ 53 F6
Rwanda *Central Africa* ▣ 52 D4
Ryukyu Islands (Ryukyu-Shoto) *Japan* ◪ 67 G6
Ryukyu-Shoto (Ryukyu Islands) *Japan* ◪ 67 G6
Rzeszów *Poland* ⊙ 20 M7

**S**
's-Gravenhage (Den Haag) (The Hague)
*Netherlands* ⊛ 17 H2
Saarbrücken *Germany* ⊙ 25 C7
Sabah *Malaysia* ▣ 70 F1
Sabkhat al Bardawil *Egypt* ◪ 42 A5
Sacramento *United States* ⊛ 84 B3
Sahara *Africa* ◪ 44 E4
Sahara-Atlas *Algeria* ▲ 47 F2
Sahel *West Africa* ◪ 50 C1
Sahyadri / Western Ghats *India* ▲ 63 B5
Sa'idabad *Iran* ⊙ 43 F2
Saigon (Ho Chi Minh) *Vietnam* ⊙ 64 D4
Saint Lawrence River *Canada* ◪ 87 G1
Saint-Denis *France* ⊙ 16 F6
Saint-Étienne *France* ⊙ 27 K8
Sakai *Japan* ⊙ 68 H6
Sakarya *Turkey* ◪ 39 E4
Salamanca *Spain* ⊙ 28 D3
Salekhard *Russia* ⊙ 21 P1
Salem *United States* ⊛ 84 B2
Salerno *Italy* ⊙ 33 J8
Saloniki (Thessaloniki) *Greece* ⊙ 36 E4
Salt Lake City *United States* ⊛ 84 D2
Salta *Argentina* ⊙ 98 H3
Salton Sea *United States* ◪ 84 D4
Salvador *Brazil* ⊙ 97 K6
Salzburg *Austria* ⊙ 31 J3
Samar *Philippines* ◪ 65 H4
Samara *Russia* ⊙ 21 L4
Samarinda *Indonesia* ⊙ 70 F3
Samarkand *Uzbekistan* ⊙ 59 M10
Samoa *Oceania* ▣ 73 J7
Samsun *Turkey* ⊙ 39 G3
San y *Yemen* ⊛ 40 D6
San Antonio *United States* ⊙ 89 G3
San Diego *United States* ⊙ 88 C2
San Francisco *United States* ⊙ 84 B3
San José *Costa Rica* ⊛ 92 H7
San Jose *United States* ⊙ 84 B3
San Luis Potosi *Mexico* ⊙ 89 E4
San Marino *Europe* ▣ 32 G5
San Miguel de Tucuman *Argentina* ⊙ 98 H4
San Salvador *El Salvador* ⊛ 92 F6
San Sebastián *Spain* ⊙ 29 J1
Sandefjord *Norway* ⊙ 19 E7
Sankt-Petersburg (St. Petersburg)
*Russia* ⊙ 20 G2
Santa Cruz *Bolivia* ⊙ 96 F7
Santa Fe *Argentina* ⊙ 98 J4
Santa Fe *United States* ⊛ 89 E1
Santander *Spain* ⊙ 28 G1
Santiago *Chile* ⊛ 98 G5
Santiago de Cuba *Cuba* ⊙ 93 J4

Santiago del Estero *Argentina* ⊙ 98 J4
Santo Domingo *Dominican Republic* ⊛ 93 L4
Santos *Brazil* ⊙ 99 M3
São Luis *Brazil* ⊙ 97 J4
São Tiago *Cape Verde* ◪ 50 (1)B2
São Paulo *Brazil* ⊛ 99 M3
São Tomé *São Tomé and Principe* ⊛ 51 F4
São Tomé and Principe *West Africa* ▣ 51 F4
Saône *France* ◪ 27 K7
Sapporo *Japan* ⊛ 69 L2
Sarajevo *Bosnia-Herzegovina* ⊛ 34 F6
Saransk *Russia* ⊙ 20 K4
Sarawak *Malaysia* ▣ 70 E2
Sardegna (Sardinia) (It.)
*Mediterranean* ◪ 33
Sardinia (Sardegna) (It.)
*Mediterranean* ◪ 33
Sargasso Sea *Central America* ◪ 93 L3
Saskatchewan *Canada* ▣ 80 K6
Sassari (Sardinia) *Italy* ⊙ 33 C8
Saudi Arabia *Middle East* ▣ 40 D4
Saurimo *Angola* ⊙ 54 C1
Saurimo *Angola* ⊙ 52 C1
Savannah *United States* ⊙ 91 E3
Savonlinna *Finland* ⊙ 18 Q6
Sawu Sea *Indonesia* ◪ 71 B4
Saynshand *Mongolia* ⊙ 66 E2
Scafell Pike *United Kingdom* ▲ 15 K7
Schwarzwald *Germany* ▲ 25 D9
Scotia Ridge *Atlantic Ocean* ◪ 99 K10
Scotia Sea *South Atlantic Ocean* ◪ 99 L10
Scotland *United Kingdom* ▣ 14 H5
Sea of Azov *Ukraine* ◪ 20 H5
Sea of Japan (Tong-Hae / Nippon-Kai)
*South East Asia* ◪ 68
Sea of Marmara (Marmara Denizi)
*Turkey* ◪ 39
Sea of Okhotsk (Hok-Kai) *East Asia* ◪ 69 M
Second-Takoradi *Ghana* ⊙ 50 D4
Segre *Spain* ◪ 29 L3
Seine *France* ◪ 26 J5
Semarang *Indonesia* ⊙ 70 E4
Semipalatinsk *Kazakhstan* ⊙ 59 P7
Sendai *Japan* ⊙ 69 L4
Sendai-Wan *Japan* ◪ 69 L4
Senegal *Mauritania* ◪ 46 C5
Senegal *West Africa* ▣ 46 B6
Seoul (South *South Korea* ⊛ 68 D5
Seram (Ceram) *Indonesia* ◪ 71 C3
Serov *Russia* ⊙ 21 N3
Serra do Mar *Brazil* ▲ 99 L4
Serra dos Parecis *Brazil* ▲ 96 E5
Sevastopol' *Ukraine* ⊙ 20 G6
Severnaya Zemlya *Russia* ◪ 58 S1
Severo-Sibirskaya Nizmennost (North Siberi
Plain) *Russia* ◪ 58
Sevilla *Spain* ⊙ 28 E7
Seychelles *Indian Ocean* ▣ 55 (2)A2
Seychelles Islands *Indian Ocean* ◪ 55 (2)C1
Sfax *Tunisia* ⊙ 47 H2
Shanghai *China* ⊙ 67 G4
Shaoxing *China* ⊙ 67 G4
Sharjah (Ash Shariqah)
*United Arab Emirates* ⊙ 43
Sheffield *United Kingdom* ⊙ 15 M8
Shenyang *China* ⊙ 67 G2
Shetland Islands *United Kingdom* ◪ 14 N1
Shijiazhuang *China* ⊙ 66 E3
Shikoku *Japan* ◪ 68 G7
Shilega *Russia* ⊙ 20 K2
Shiraz *Iran* ⊙ 43 E2
Shizuoka *Japan* ⊙ 69 K6
Shkodër *Albania* ⊙ 36 B2
Shreveport *United States* ⊙ 90 C3
Siauliai *Lithuania* ⊙ 19 M9
Siberia *Russia* ◪ 58 M4
Sibiu *Romania* ⊙ 35 M4
Sibuyan Sea *Philippines* ◪ 65 G4
Sicilia (Sicily) *Italy* ◪ 33 H11
Sicilian Channel *Italy* ◪ 33 F11
Sicily (Sicilia) *Italy* ◪ 33 H11
Sierra Leone *West Africa* ▣ 50 B3
Sierra Madre Occidental *Mexico* ▲ 92 D3

ra Madre Oriental *Mexico* 92 D4
ra Morena *Spain* 28 B3
ra Nevada *United States* 84 B3
ote-Ain *Russia* 60 N8
pson Desert *Australia* 75 G5
al *Egypt* 42 A6
agore *Asia* 70 C2
apore *Singapore* 70 C2
iju *North Korea* 68 C3
cusa (Syracuse) *Sicily* 33 K11
a (Surt) *Libya* 48 B1
ema *Central Japan* 28 D4
tas *Turkey* 39 G4
tsy *Russia* 19 Q7
rekan *Norway / Denmark* 19 D8
gerak *Norway / Denmark*
llefteå *Sweden* 18 L4
lopje *Macedonia* 36 D2
ntsy *Russia* 19 Q7
vakia *Europe* 23 H9
venia *Europe* 34 H5
dederevo *Yugoslavia* 34 H5
polensk *Russia* 20 G4
lyana (Izmir) *Turkey* 39 G4
wdon *United Kingdom* 15 J9
wdonia *United Kingdom* 15 J9
chi (Soci) *Russia* 39 H2
i (Sochi) *Russia* 39 H2
iety Islands (Fr. Poly.) *Oceania* 73 L7
otra *Yemen* 41 F7
ia Marita *Finland* 18 P3
omon Islands *Oceania* 72 G6
way Firth *United Kingdom* 15 J9
alia *Central Africa* 53 H3
hes *Hungary / Romania* 35 L2
mone *Poland* 23 J7
al (Seoul) *South Korea* 68 D5
th Africa *Southern Africa* 54 D6
th Australia *Australia* 74 F5
th Carolina *United States* 91 E3
th China Sea (Nan Hai) *China* 65 E3
th Dakota *United States* 85 F2
th Downs *United Kingdom* 16 C4
th East Cape *Australia* 75 J8
th Georgia *South Atlantic Ocean* 99 P9
th Island *New Zealand* 77 B6
th Korea *South East Asia* 68 D5
th Pole Plateau *Antarctica* 100 (2)LL1
th Taranaki Bight *New Zealand* 76 D4
th West Pacific Basin *Oceania* 73 L9
thampton *United Kingdom* 16 M10
thend-on-Sea *United Kingdom* 16 D3
thern Alps *New Zealand* 77 B7
thern Ocean *Australia* 100 (2)Y3
thern Uplands *United Kingdom* 14 J6
thwest Cape *New Zealand* 77 A8
tian *Europe* 26 P5
encer Gulf *Australia* 75 G6
zbergen *Norway* 56 F1
it *Croatia* 34 D6
kane *United States* 84 C1
ingfield (Illinois) *United States* 86 C3
ingfield (Missouri) *United States* 86 B3
ingfield (Oregon) *United States* 84 B2
dinny Khrebet *Russia* 61 T6
ndnesibirskoye Ploskogorn (Central Siberian Plain) *Russia* 60 F4
anka *Indian Ocean* 63 D7
David's Head *United Kingdom* 15 H10
George's Channel *United Kingdom* 15 G10
Croatia 34 D6
Helena Bay *South Africa* 54 B8
John's *Canada* 81 W7
Kitts-Nevis *Caribbean* 93 M5
Lawrence Seaway *Canada* 87 F1
Louis *United States* 86 B3
Lucia *Caribbean* 93 M6

St. Paul *United States* 86 B2
St. Petersburg (Sankt-Peterburg) *Russia* 20 G2
St. Pierre and Miquelon (Fr.) *North Atlantic Ocean* 81 V7
St. Vincent and The Grenadines *Caribbean* 93 M6
Stanley *Falkland Islands* 99 K9
Stara Planina *Yugoslavia / Bulgaria* 35 K6
Stara Zagora *Bulgaria* 35 N7
Stavanger *Norway* 19 C7
Stavropol' *Russia* 20 J5
Stenón Karpathou *Greece* 37 K8
Stettin (Szczecin) *Poland* 22 D4
Stewart Island *New Zealand* 77 A8
Stockholm *Sweden* 19 K7
Stockton *United States* 84 B3
Strait of Bonifacio *Europe* 33 C7
Strait of Dover *United Kingdom / France* 15 E4
Strait of Gibraltar *Spain / Morocco* 28 D9
Strait of Hormuz *Middle East* 43 F3
Strait of Malacca *Asia* 70 C2
Straits of Florida *United States* 91 E5
Strasbourg *France* 26 N5
Strimon *Bulgaria / Greece* 36 F3
Struma *Bulgaria / Greece* 36 F3
Stuttgart *Germany* 25 E8
Stykkishólmur *Iceland* 18 (1)B2
Sucre *Bolivia* 96 D7
Sudan *Central Africa* 48 E4
Sudan *Central Africa* 50 D2
Sudeten (Sudety) *Poland* 23 E7
Sudety (Sudeten) *Poland* 23 E7
Suez Canal *Egypt* 49 F1
Sulawesi (Celebes) *Indonesia* 71 A3
Sulu Archipelago *Philippines* 65 F5
Sulu Sea *South East Asia* 65 F5
Sumatra (Sumatra) *Indonesia* 70 C3
Sumatra (Sumatra) *Indonesia* 70 C3
Sumba *Indonesia* 71 C4
Sumbawanga *Tanzania* 52 E5
Sumy *Ukraine* 20 G4
Surabaya *Indonesia* 70 E4
Surakarta *Malaysia* 70 E4
Surat *India* 64 B4
Surgut *Russia* 58 N5
Surinam *South America* 97 F2
Surt (Sirte) *Libya* 48 B1
Suwon *South Korea* 68 D5
Svalbard *Norway* 100 (2)P2
Sveg *Sweden* 19 H5
Swansea *United Kingdom* 15 J10
Swaziland *Southern Africa* 55 E5
Sweden *Europe* 18 H5
Swindon *United Kingdom* 16 C3
Switzerland *Europe* 30 C4
Sydney *Australia* 75 P7
Syktyvkar *Russia* 20 J3
Syracuse (Siracusa) *Sicily* 33 K11
Syria *Middle East* 42 D2
Syrian Desert (Badiet esh Sham) *Syria* 42 E3
Syzran' *Russia* 21 K4
Szczecin (Stettin) *Poland* 22 D4
Szeged *Hungary* 23 K11

**T**

T'ai-pei *Taiwan* 65 G2
Tabriz *Iran* 39 M4
Tacoma *United States* 84 B1
Tadzjikistan *Asia* 41 J2
Taebaek-Sanmaek *North Korea / South Korea* 68 D4
Taegu *South Korea* 68 E6
Taehan-Haehyop (Korea Strait) *South Korea / Japan* 68 D7
Taejon *North Korea* 68 D5
Taiwan *South East Asia* 65 G2
Taiwan Strait *Taiwan / China* 65 F2
Taiyuan *China* 66 E3
Tallahassee *United States* 91 E3
Tallinn *Estonia* 19 N7
Tamale *Ghana* 50 D3
Tambov *Russia* 20 J4

Tammerfors (Tampere) *Finland* 19 M6
Tampa *United States* 91 E4
Tampere (Tammerfors) *Finland* 19 M6
Tangier (Tanger) *Morocco* 46 D1
Tangier (Tanger) *Morocco* 46 D1
Tanzania *Central Africa* 53 E5
Taoudenni *Mali* 46 E4
Tarabulus (Tripoli) *Libya* 48 B1
Taranto *Italy* 33 M8
Tarim Basin *China* 59 Q10
Tarko-Sale *Russia* 21 R2
Tårnaby *Sweden* 18 H4
Tarnow *Poland* 23 L7
Tartu *Estonia* 19 P7
Tashauz *Turkmenistan* 59 K9
Tashkent *Uzbekistan* 59 M9
Tasikmalaya *Indonesia* 70 D4
Tasman Sea *Australia* 75 K7
Tasmania *Australia* 75 J8
Tatarskiy Proliv *Russia* 61 Q7
Taurus *Germany* 25 E6
Tbilisi (Tiflis) *Georgia* 39 S3
Tegucigalpa *Honduras* 93 G6
Tehran (Tehran) *Iran* 40 E2
Tehran (Tehran) *Iran* 40 E2
Tel Aviv-Yafo (Jaffa) *Israel* 42 B4
Temuco *Chile* 98 B6
Ten Degree Channel *Andaman Islands and Nicobar* 63 F7
Ténéré *Niger* 47 G5
Tennessee *United States* 86 C3
Teresina *Brazil* 97 J5
Ternopol' *Ukraine* 20 F5
Texas *United States* 90 B3
Thabana Ntlenyana *Lesotho* 54 D5
Thailand *South East Asia* 67 B5
Thames *United Kingdom* 15 F10
The Everglades *United States* 91 E4
The Gulf *Middle East* 43 C2
The Hague ('s-Gravenhage) (Den Haag) *Netherlands* 17 H2
The Solent *United Kingdom* 15 P8
The Wash *United Kingdom* 15 P8
Thessaloniki (Saloniki) *Greece* 36 E4
Thimphu *Bhutan* 63 S3
Thrakikó Pélagos *Greece* 36 G4
Three Kings Islands *New Zealand* 76 C2
Thunder Bay *Canada* 87 F4
Thüringer Wald *Germany* 25 F6
Tianjin *China* 66 F3
Tibesti *Chad* 48 C3
Tibet *China* 62 D2
Tien Shan *China* 59 Q9
Tiflis (Tbilisi) *Georgia* 39 S3
Tigris (Dijlah) *Middle East* 43 B1
Tijuana *Mexico* 92 A2
Tilburg *Netherlands* 17 J3
Timisoara *Romania* 34 J4
Timor Sea *South East Asia* 71 C5
Tinaca Point *Philippines* 65 G5
Tindouf *Algeria* 46 D3
Tirana (Tiranë) *Albania* 36 B3
Tirane (Tirana) *Albania* 36 B3
Tiraspol' *Moldova* 35 S3
Tîrgu Mures *Romania* 35 M3
Togo *West Africa* 50 E4
Tokelau (N.Z.) *Oceania* 73 J6
Tokyo *Japan* 69 K6
Tombouctou *Mali* 46 E5
Tomsk *Russia* 59 R6
Tong-Hae / Nippon-Kai (Sea of Japan) *South East Asia* 68 G4
Tonga *Oceania* 73 J7
Tonga Islands (Tonga) *Oceania* 73 J8
Topeka *United States* 86 A3
Torino (Turin) *Italy* 32 B3
Tornio *Finland* 18 N4
Toronto *Canada* 81 Q8
Torun *Poland* 22 J6
Torquay *United Kingdom* 15 K11
Torreón *Mexico* 92 D3
Toulon *France* 27 M10
Toulouse *France* 27 G10

Tourcoing *France* ● 16 G4
Tours *France* ● 26 F6
Toyama-Wan *Japan* 🏳 69 J5
Trâblous (Tripoli) *Lebanon* 🏳 42 C2
Trent *United Kingdom* 🏳 15 M9
Trenton *United States* ● 87 F2
Trier *Germany* ● 17 K5
Trieste *Italy* ● 32 H3
Trinidad and Tobago *Caribbean* ▲ 93 N6
Tripoli (Tarabulus) *Libya* ● 48 H2
Tripoli (Trâblous) *Lebanon* ● 42 C2
Tripolis *Greece* ● 36 E7
Trofors *Norway* ● 18 G4
Troitsko-Pechorsk *Russia* ● 21 M2
Trondheim *Norway* ● 18 F5
Troyes *France* ● 26 K5
Trujillo *Peru* ● 96 B5
Tsugaru-Kaikyo *Japan* 🏳 69 L3
Tsushima-Kaikyo (Korea Strait)
        *South Korea / Japan* 🏳 68 D7
Tuamotu Archipelago (Fr. Poly.)
        *Oceania* 🏳 73 M7
Tubruq *Libya* ● 48 D1
Tubuai Islands (Fr. Poly.) *Oceania* 🏳 73 L8
Tucson *United States* ● 89 D2
Tula *Russia* ● 20 H4
Tulsa *United States* ● 90 B2
Tunis *Tunisia* ● 47 H1
Tunisia *North Africa* ▲ 47 G2
Turin (Torino) *Italy* ● 32 B3
Turkey *Europe* ▲ 39 F4
Turkmenistan *Asia* ▲ 41 G2
Turku / Åbo *Finland* ● 19 L6
Tuvalu *Oceania* ▲ 72 H6
Tver' *Russia* ● 20 G3
Tyan' Shan *China* ▲ 59 Q9
Tyrrhenian Sea (Mare Tirreno) *Italy* 🏳 33 G9

**U**

Uddevalla *Sweden* ● 19 F7
Udine *Italy* ● 31 J4
Ufa *Russia* ● 21 M4
Uganda *Central Africa* ▲ 53 E3
Ujung Pandang *Indonesia* ● 71 A4
Ukraine *Europe* ▲ 20 G5
Ulaanbaatar *Mongolia* ● 60 H7
Ulan-Ude *Russia* ● 60 H6
Ulsan *South Korea* ● 68 E6
Umeå *Sweden* ● 18 K5
United Arab Emirates *Middle East* ▲ 43 E5
United Kingdom *Europe* ▲ 14 M5
United States *North America* ▲ 82 F4
Uppsala *Sweden* ● 19 H7
Ural Mountains (Ural'skiy Khrebet)
        *Russia* 🏳 21 M3
Ural'sk *Kazakhstan* ● 21 L4
Ural'skiy Khrebet (Ural Mountains)
        *Russia* 🏳 21 M3
Uranium City *Canada* ● 80 K5
Uruguay *South America* ▲ 99 K5
Uruguay *Uruguay* 🏳 99 K5
Ürümqi *China* ● 59 R9
Ust-Ilimsk *Russia* ● 60 G5
Ust-Isil'ma *Russia* ● 21 L1
Utah *United States* 🏳 84 D3
Utrecht *Netherlands* ● 17 J2
Utsunomiya *Japan* ● 69 K5
Uzbekistan *Asia* ▲ 59 L9
Uzhgorod *Ukraine* ● 35 K1

**V**

Vadodara *India* ● 41 K5
Vadsø *Norway* ● 18 Q1
Vaduz *Liechtenstein* ■ 30 E3
Valencia *Spain* ● 29 F5
Valladolid *Spain* ● 28 F3
Vallée du Tilemsi *Mali* 🏳 47 F5
Valletta *Malta* ■ 33 J7
Valmiera *Latvia* ● 19 N8
Valparaiso *Chile* ● 98 C5
Van Gölu *Turkey* 🏳 39 K4
Vanuatu *Oceania* ▲ 72 G7

Varanasi *India* ● 62 D3
Varna *Bulgaria* ● 35 Q6
Västerås *Sweden* ● 19 J7
Vatican City *Europe* ▲ 32 G7
Vatnajökull *Iceland* 🏳 18 (1)E2
Växjö *Sweden* ● 19 H8
Vel'sk *Russia* ● 20 J2
Velebit *Croatia* 🏳 34 C5
Venezia (Venice) *Italy* ● 32 G3
Venezuela *South America* ▲ 96 D2
Venice (Venezia) *Italy* ● 32 G3
Verdun *France* ● 17 K6
Verhovina *Ukraine* ● 35 M1
Vermont *United States* 🏳 87 F2
Vernon *France* ● 16 E5
Verona *Italy* ● 32 E3
Versailles *France* ● 16 F6
Vesterålen *Norway* 🏳 18 H2
Vesuvio *Italy* ▲ 33 J8
Viangchan (Vientiane) *Laos* ■ 64 C4
Vicenza *Italy* ● 31 J7
Victoria *Canada* 🏳 80 G7
Victoria Canada ● 80 G7
Victoria Falls *Southern Africa* ● 54 D3
Victoria Island *Canada* 🏳 80 K2
Victoria Nile *Uganda* 🏳 53 E3
Vienna (Wien) *Austria* ■ 31 M2
Vientiane (Viangchan) *Laos* ■ 64 C4
Vietnam *South East Asia* ▲ 64 C2
Vigo *Spain* ● 28 B2
Vik *Iceland* ● 18 (1)D3
Vilnius *Lithuania* ■ 19 N9
Vinson Massif *Antarctica* ▲ 100 (3)JJ2
Virful Moldoveanu *Romania* ▲ 35 M4
Virgin Islands (U.K.) *Caribbean* 🏳 93 M5
Virgin Islands (U.S.) *Caribbean* 🏳 93 M5
Virginia *United States* 🏳 87 E3
Virginia Beach *United States* ● 87 E3
Virovitica *Croatia* ● 34 E4
Visayan Sea *Philippines* 🏳 65 G4
Vishakhapatnam *India* ● 63 D5
Vistula (Wisla) *Poland* 🏳 22 H4
Vitebsk *Belarus* ● 20 G3
Vitória *Brazil* ● 97 G4
Vitorog *Bosnia-Herzegovina* ▲ 34 D5
Vladikavkaz *Russia* ● 39 L2
Vladivostok *Russia* ● 60 N8
Volga *Russia* 🏳 21 K4
Volgograd *Russia* ● 20 J5
Vóries Sporádes (Northern Sporades)
        *Greece* 🏳 36 F6
Vorkuta *Russia* ● 58 L4
Voronezh *Russia* ● 20 H4
Vostocno-Sibirskoye More (East Siberian Sea)
        *Russia* 🏳 61 T2
Vuktyl *Russia* ● 21 M2

**W**

Waco *United States* ● 90 B3
Wad Medani *Sudan* ● 49 F5
Waddeneilanden *Netherlands* 🏳 17 H1
Waddenzee *Netherlands* 🏳 17 J1
Waitaki River *New Zealand* 🏳 77 C7
Wake (U.S.) *Oceania* 🏳 72 G3
Waku-Kungo *Angola* ● 52 B6
Wales *United Kingdom* 🏳 15 J9
Wallis and Futuna (Fr.) *Oceania* 🏳 73 J7
Warsaw (Warszawa) *Poland* ■ 22 L5
Warszawa (Warsaw) *Poland* ■ 22 L5
Washington *United States* 🏳 84 B1
Washington D.C. *United States* ■ 87 E3
Weddell Sea *Antarctica* 🏳 100 (2)A2
Wellesley Islands *Australia* 🏳 75 G3
Wellington *New Zealand* ■ 77 E5
Wenzhou *China* ● 67 G5
West Siberian Plain (Zapadno-Sibirskaya
        Ravnina) *Russia* 🏳 58 N5
West Virginia *United States* 🏳 87 D3
Westalpen *France* ▲ 30 B6
Western Australia *Australia* 🏳 74 B4
Western Sahara (Morocco)
        *West Africa* ▲ 46 C4
Whakatane *New Zealand* ● 76 F3
White Sea (Beloye More) *Russia* 🏳 20 H1

Whitehorse *Canada* ● 80 D4
Wichita *United States* ● 90 B2
Wichita Falls *United States* ● 89 B3
Wicklow Mountains *Ireland* ▲ 15 G9
Wien (Vienna) *Austria* ■ 31 M2
Wiesbaden *Germany* ● 25 D6
Windhoek *Namibia* ■ 54 B4
Windward Islands *Caribbean* 🏳 93 M6
Winnipeg *Canada* ● 80 M7
Wisconsin *United States* 🏳 86 B2
Wisla (Vistula) *Poland* 🏳 22 H4
Wollongong *Australia* ● 75 K6
Wroclaw (Breslau) *Poland* ● 23 G6
Wuhan *China* ● 66 E4
Wuppertal *Germany* ● 25 C5
Wyoming *United States* 🏳 85 E2
Wyzyna Lubelska *Poland* 🏳 23 M6

**X**

Xi'an *China* ● 66 D4
Xi Jiang *China* 🏳 66 E6

**Y**

Yakutsk *Russia* ● 60 M4
Yalinga *Central African Republic* ● 52 C2
Yam Ha Melah (Dead Sea) *Israel* 🏳 42 C5
Yam Kinneret (Lake Tiberias) *Israel* 🏳 42 C4
Yambol *Bulgaria* ● 35 P7
Yamoussoukro *Côte D'Ivoire* ■ 50 C3
Yangon (Rangoon) *Myanmar (Burma)* ● 64 B3
Yaoundé *Cameroon* ■ 51 G4
Yekaterinburg *Russia* ● 21 N3
Yellow Sea (Huang Hai / Hwang-Hae)
        *South East Asia* 🏳 67 ...
Yellowknife *Canada* ● 80 J4
Yemen *Middle East* ▲ 40 E7
Yenisey *Russia* 🏳 58 R4
Yenisey Skiy Kryazh *Russia* ▲ 58 T6
Yerevan *Armenia* ■ 39 L3
Yerushalayim (Jerusalem) *Israel* ■ 42 C5
Ylivieska *Finland* ● 18 M4
Yogyakarta *Malaysia* ● 70 E4
Yokohama *Japan* ● 69 K6
Yokosuka *Japan* ● 69 K6
York *United Kingdom* ● 15 M7
Yoshkar Ola *Russia* ● 21 K3
Yucatan Channel *Mexico* 🏳 93 G4
Yugoslavia *Europe* ▲ 34 G6
Yukon Territory *Canada* 🏳 80 D4
Yuzhno Sakhalinsk *Russia* ● 61 Q7

**Z**

Zagreb *Croatia* ■ 34 C4
Zagros Mountains *Iran* ▲ 43 D1
Zaire Democratic Republic of Congo ✦ 52 C3
Zambezi *Southern Africa* 🏳 54 C3
Zambia *Southern Africa* ▲ 54 C3
Zamboanga *Philippines* ● 65 G5
Zanzibar *Tanzania* ● 53 F5
Zanzibar *Tanzania* 🏳 53 F5
Západné Karpaty (Carpathians)
        *Poland / Slovakia* ▲ 23 ...
Zapadno-Sibirskaya Ravnina (West Siberian
        Plain) *Russia* 🏳 58 ...
Zaragoza *Spain* ● 29 K3
Zentral Alpen *Switzerland* ▲ 30 D4
Zhangjiakou *China* ● 66 F2
Zhengzhou *China* ● 66 E3
Zibo *China* ● 66 F3
Zigong *China* ● 66 C5
Zimbabwe *Southern Africa* ▲ 54 D3
Zouërat *Mauritania* ● 46 C4
Zrenjanin *Yugoslavia* ● 34 H4
Zürich *Switzerland* ● 30 D3

# World physical, Pacific centred